PERSPECTIVES ON
PERCIVAL EVERETT

PERSPECTIVES ON

Percival
Everett

Edited by Keith B. Mitchell and
Robin G. Vander

UNIVERSITY PRESS OF MISSISSIPPI / JACKSON

www.upress.state.ms.us

Designed by Peter D. Halverson

The University Press of Mississippi is a member of the Association of American
University Presses.

First printing 2013

∞

Library of Congress Cataloging-in-Publication Data

Perspectives on Percival Everett / edited by Keith B. Mitchell and Robin G.
Vander.
p. cm. — (Margaret Walker Alexander series in African American studies)
Includes bibliographical references and index.
ISBN 978-1-61703-682-8 (cloth: alk. paper) — ISBN 978-1-61703-683-5 (ebook)
1. Everett, Percival L.—Criticism and interpretation. I. Mitchell, Keith B., 1962-
II. Vander, Robin G.
PS3555.V34Z85 2013
813'.54—dc23   2012021646

British Library Cataloging-in-Publication Data available

Contents

Acknowledgments

Keith: I would like to acknowledge the amazing folks at the Virginia Foundation for the Humanities who, in the summer of 2010, gave me time, space, and tremendous resources to work on this project. I would also like to thank my friends and colleagues in the Department of English at the University of Massachusetts, Lowell. In particular, I would like to thank my chair, Professor Anthony Szczeisul, for simply being there. His presence makes all the difference in the world. In addition, my conversations with Professors Jonathan Silverman, Michael Millner, Todd Tiechten, and Todd Avery gave me pause to even more deeply consider my role as teacher, scholar, and colleague, especially in light of their own rigorous standards of excellence. Last, but never least, I am grateful to Ms. Paula Haines and Professors Melissa Pennell, Marlow Miller, Jeannie Judge, Laura Barefield, Shelley Barish, and Sue Kim for their unwavering support and friendship.

Robin: I am deeply grateful to my colleagues in the Department of English at Xavier University of Louisiana and to those across the campus in Communication Studies and in Art who continuously offer their support and encouragement. My department chair, Professor Nicole P. Greene, was instrumental in making sure that I had time to pursue this project and others, and that my research and teaching were given space to grow. Professor Bonnie Jo Noonan provided friendship, constructive critiques, and a detailed eye for the practice of smart and accessible writing. Her sheer joy for teaching and writing are inspiring. My conversations with Mora Beauchamp-Byrd, Kimberly Chandler, Monique Guillory, and Ross Louis continuously opened intellectual doors for me to keep moving forward. Lastly, to Professors Thaddeo Babiiha, Violet Bryan, and Ronald Dorris—I respectfully remain the acorn among the oaks.

The editors, collectively, wish to thank the contributors to *Perspectives on Percival Everett* for their scholarship, commitment, and patience in developing this project. We are indebted to the editors and staff at the University Press of Mississippi, in particular, Walter Biggins for believing in this project from its inception and to Anne Stascavage for working closely with us to bring it to fruition. We also appreciate the thoughtful care provided by our copyeditor, Debbie Upton. Lastly, our utmost appreciation goes to Professor Percival Everett for such a compelling literary and artistic career and for his abiding support of this particular project in art and spirit.

Changing the Frame, Framing the Change
The Art of Percival Everett

KEITH B. MITCHELL AND ROBIN G. VANDER

So we must keep trying anything and everything, improvising, borrowing from others, developing from others, dialectically using one text as comment upon another, schematizing, using the incentive to new wanderings, returning from these excursions to schematize again, being oversubtle when the straining seems to promise some further glimpse, and making amends by reduction to some very simple anecdote. —KENNETH BURKE

To say that Percival Everett is one of the most accomplished and prolific contemporary *African American* writers is also to say that Percival Everett is one of the most accomplished and prolific *American* writers. He is the author of eighteen novels, three collections of short fiction, three collections of poetry, and a children's book. Born in 1956 in Fort Gordon, a small military base in Augusta, Georgia, he was primarily raised in South Carolina. Everett received his M.A. in fiction from Brown University in 1982, and was an associate professor at the University of Kentucky from 1985 to 1988, and a full professor at the University of Notre Dame from 1988 to 1991. He is currently Distinguished Professor of English at the University of Southern California. Since the publication of his first novel, *Suder*, in 1983, he has been the recipient of numerous awards and accolades. These include the New American Writing Award for *Zulus* in 1990; the Hillsdale Award; the Fellowship of Southern Writers (2001); the Hurston/Wright Legacy Award for *Erasure* (2002); the American Academy of Arts and Letters Literature Award (2003); the PEN USA Literary Award (2006–2007); and the Dos Passos Prize in Literature, the Charles Angoff Award, the Premio Vallambrosa

Gregor von Rezzori Prize (Italy), the Hurston/Wright Legacy Award, and the Believer Book Award, all received in 2010. Everett's literary production has been impressive; on average, he has managed to publish at least one novel per year since 1983. One would imagine that most writers who might produce such a large body of creative work would suffer from a decline in imaginative and innovative faculties; however, this is not the case with Percival Everett. Everett never crosses the same river twice. He has experimented with and mastered the art of creative expression in many different literary genres that sends the reader on rollicking rollercoaster rides: dizzying and thrilling, and ultimately immensely satisfying. One need only read his work to see the topical, stylistic, and narrative range of his literary output: *Suder*, about an ageing African American baseball player on an existential quest for wholeness; *Zulus* (1990), a post-apocalyptic, satirical novel that echoes Lewis Carroll's *Alice in Wonderland*; *The Water Cure* (2007), a subtle indictment of post-911 American politics during the Bush administration; *I Am Not Sidney Poitier* (2009), a narrative that interrogates the very nature of subjectivity; and *Assumption* (2011), a mind-bending detective story that questions our reliance on inductive and deductive reason to explain and understand the world; the wellspring of his imagination runs deep, indeed.

Despite, however, the praise and overwhelmingly positive critical reception that Everett and his work have garnered, there has been an astounding dearth of critical and scholarly examination of his fiction. The lack on the part of scholars in African American *and* American literary and cultural studies has been nothing less than scandalous. Indeed, it is safe to say that Everett's work is arguably better known in Europe than here in the United States. To date, scholars in France have published two collections of essays on his fiction: *Percival Everett: Transatlantic Readings* (2007), edited by Claire Maniez and Anne-Laure Tissut, and *Reading Percival Everett, European Perspectives: Symposium de Tours* (2007), edited by Claude Julien. At this date, only the Maniez and Tissut collection remains in print. Neither in Europe nor the United States has there been a monogram published on his work. This collection of essays, we feel, is a necessary and timely intervention and is an important critical starting point for scholars both familiar and unfamiliar with his work.

Percival Everett and the Politics of (Black) Identity

If, as Jon Woodson claims, black poetry, specifically, and black literature, generally, in artistic representations of black experiences in the past enacted a "resubjectification of the black self," Everett and other post-civil rights authors have enacted a *revision* of the resubjectification of the black self in which identifacatory multiplicity is the sociopolitical aim (Spencer 72–73). We have seen this in the case of writers as diverse as Toni Morrison, Clarence Major, Charles Johnson, John Edgar Wideman, Gloria Naylor, Edward P. Jones, Colson Whitehead, Jerome Beatty, and Martha Southgate, among others. Many of these writers deal with middle-class black experiences as much as experiences of the folk. Moreover, many of these writers have built upon and expanded the African American literary tradition by taking up narrative forms and subject matter that have heretofore not been readily advanced in the literature. Often literary critics have attempted to categorize these African American writers as "experimental writers," which at best meant that they employ innovative narrative techniques to portray black experiences in their fiction and at worst that these innovative narrative techniques somehow make their work "less black" due to the work's supposed difficulty and black "inauthenticity." The latter charge is meant to imply that because the work was "avant-garde" (whatever that is supposed to mean), African American readers could not identify with the characters and/or situations rendered in these texts. This often meant that black and white critics alike were quick to dismiss these "experimental writers'" literary efforts as perhaps too indulgent to suit the tastes of the general (black) reading public or to satisfy black and white critics' expectations for "authentic" black fiction. It has only been in the last ten years that serious critical work has begun to appear on African American "experimental writers" like Major and Wideman, and it is only now that younger writers such as Beatty, Whitehead, and Southgate are beginning to receive serious critical attention; much more needs to be done. The dearth of scholarly work on African American writers who do not necessarily fit certain prescribed formal or thematic categorizations deemed as "black" are often relegated to the margins of African American literary history, tradition, and critical engagement (we see this in the poetry *and* the fiction). Perhaps what problematizes Percival Everett's writing for readers and critics, even more than his formal narrative innovation, is his refusal as an African American writer to be categorized at all. Despite the experimental nature of Morrison's, Johnson's, Major's, and Wideman's creative work, their art is rooted in arguably more readily identifiable black experiences and black expression. For example, unlike the aforementioned African American writers, Everett rarely employs African American vernacular speech patterns in the delineation of his characters. This is perhaps where one finds Everett's unique authorial voice majorly departing from other African American writers of his generation and of the past. In an interview Everett points out that he simply wants to be viewed as a writer who happens to be black and not an African American writer, per se, with all of the historical, cultural, and racial baggage that accompanies the term. This, ironically, he feels, allows him a much wider imaginative latitude in his artistic expression of black experiences. In an interview with Anthony Stewart, Everett castigates the commercial manipulations of the publishing industry and the imperceptive vision of the average reader that often forces African American writers to write about subject matter and render character types that have been deemed "blacker" than others:

> PE: Being black in America, you're exotic in certain places and certain times. You're exotic if you're in New York and you're brown and you happen to be a Cheyenne Indian. But if you're black, "you're not exotic, we're used to you." You're exotic in that awful way if you show up at a fancy party and you're the only black person there. But on the street, you're not exotic. And the same would be true of white Americans who wander into a party full of black people. But they're not exotic. They're simply out of place. And that's how it's perceived, by everyone. It's a wonderfully fucked up culture we live in.
>
> AS: The difference between being exotic and of being out of place. Being exotic is something that somebody else can put to good use. Right? You can sell exoticism in a way that maybe you can't sell out of place.
>
> PE: Exactly, which is why the easy road for American publishing has been to publish novels about black farmers or inner-city, you know
> . . .

AS: Slaves.

PE: And slaves. Because these are pictures [of blackness] that are easily
commodified. But if it's the black middle class, and it's so different
from someone else's, then what's exotic about that? (Stewart 299)

Thus as counternarratives to what he sees as the myopic vision of mainstream publishers and the reading public, the protagonists in Everett's
novels, racially identified and otherwise, are ranchers, hydrologists, baseball players, doctors, romance writers, Vietnam veterans, cowboys, Greek
gods, child savants, and serial killers. This, however, is not to advance that
Percival Everett rejects his African American roots; rather, Everett has made
a career of writing against proscriptions of black representations in his fiction—that black writers have to represent a kind of universalized, monolithic black experience in order for their art to be considered legitimately
black. Thus, we see with Everett instances where race, subject matter, narrative form, and other innovations *appear* not to have much of anything to
do with the lives of African Americans. We emphasize "appear" because if
one closely interrogates Everett's oeuvre, as the extraordinary contributors
to this collection have, one would find themes, images, motifs, and intertextual references that connect his fiction well within *as well as* outside of
the African American literary tradition. Everett's fiction invariably speaks
b(l)ack to innovative fiction writers such as Jean Toomer, Zora Neale Hurston, George Schuyler, Richard Wright, and Ralph Ellison, often through
biting parody and satire. Everett signifies, again often through parody and
satire, upon numerous Euro-American writers, artists, philosophers, and
literary theorists to show that what might appear not to be of any value
to nor concern for African Americans has absolutely always preoccupied
African American artistic, social, and political expression. And in doing
so, Everett raises even more complicated questions concerning African
American identity and culture in the twenty-first century. As this collection proves, Everett's work is more than black enough; his work embraces
the universality of what it means to be human, regardless of race. In short,
like his literary ancestor, Ralph Ellison, to whom he owes much, Everett's
extraordinary body of work demonstrates what Ellison figured out over six-
ty-five years ago in the writing of *Invisible Man* (1947); that in the creation
of "authentic" African American fiction, "black is an' black ain't . . . ."

Perspectives on Percival Everett is but one measured reflection on Everett's career as an accomplished and prolific writer of the twentieth and twenty-first centuries, and of the author's own critiques of identity politics and race situated at the intersection of literary theory and creative writing. In this collection Everett's novels, short fiction, and poetry are analyzed and given thoughtful consideration as to their representation of physical bodies socially defined as "black" yet transcending, disturbing, and interrogating any and all meanings and meaningful applications of the term and its purported markers. Herein, the essays reflect upon Everett's critique of social discourse and his immersion in theoretical praxis, the place and displacement of definitions in constructing identity. If we are to state, emphatically no less, that Percival Everett is one of the most accomplished and prolific writers of his generation, then *Perspectives on Percival Everett* intimates the limitless theoretical lenses one might appropriate in reading his work and the myriad intersections that continue to reveal themselves to us: from Russian Formalism to Structuralism, Psychoanalytic to Critical Race Theory, Performance-based Analysis and Reader-Response. Throughout the collection, Everett's interest in identity as formed through language and the materiality of the body, form the foundation for how contributors discuss the author's engagement with proposed cinematic adaptations of his work, the evolution of interpretive communities for his work and those imagined within, and how racial and cultural reality take shape.

In "'knowledge^2 + certainty^2 = squat^2': (re)Thinking Identity and Meaning in Percival Everett's *The Water Cure*," Jonathan Dittman discusses the Russian Formalist technique of "defamiliarization" and the performative act of naming. The role of language as a signifier for culture and cultural identity is interrogated by Dittman's analysis of the novel's protagonist, Ishmael Kidder, an African American male romance writer who appropriates a woman's name and identity. The essay also examines the novel's postmodern critique of absolute truths.

Sarah Mantilla Griffin extends the considerations of language and identity in the essay "'This Strange Juggler's Game': Forclusion in Percival Everett's *I Am Not Sidney Poitier*," providing a psychoanalytic reading of the novel *I Am Not Sidney Poitier* (2009) through the use of Lacan and the absent signifier. Moving beyond a mere analysis of lacking the father figure, Mantilla Griffin addresses the importance of naming within African

American culture and the complexities that arise through the disconnection of the linguistic concept and sound-image.

Literary and cultural theories are inherently at work in Everett's writing and are continuously reflected throughout his writing. Ronald Dorris acknowledges Everett as a scholar by introducing a new means of textual analysis in his discussion of the novel *Frenzy* (1997). The essay, "*Frenzy*: Framing Text to Set Discourse in a Cultural Continuum," entails a close reading of Everett's use of Euripides's *The Bacchae* as a narrative frame in order to make insightful cross-generic connections, on a literary and cultural continuum, between Afro-Asiatic and Greek mythopoesis.

With "The Preservationist Impulse in Percival Everett's 'True Romance,'" contributor Frédéric Dumas shifts attention from novels to short fiction and begins to expand the discussion of how the African American community traditionally has been depicted in literature, particularly, in regards to the issues and concerns that have garnered the community's attention and resources. In his essay, Dumas highlights Everett's illustration of African Americans' interests in environmental concerns and the author's situating the community along the landscape of the American Southwest. While these representations clearly exhibit an expansion of how readers might view the community, Dumas still discusses archetypal tropes in Everett's works including the author's use of the male figure enlisting a female identity for a pseudonym, a similar analysis found earlier in Dittman's discussion of *The Water Cure* (2007). Another recurring theme in Everett's work will be that of the author's critique of the contemporary publishing world and other modes of artistic production that Everett believes seek to pigeonhole and stifle broader and more inclusive African American artistic expressions.

"The Mind-Body Split in *American Desert*: Synthesizing Everett's Critique of Race, Religion, and Science" problematizes racial determinism and essentialism by exploring the post-Cartesian split. Critiquing religion, government, corporations, and media, contributor Richard Schur analyzes discursive formation and the role institutions assume in shaping reality and identity within societies. Arguing for the limitations of knowing through science and media, Schur's essay thoughtfully considers the consequences when institutionalized ways of knowing fail to explain what it means to be alive.

Uzzie Cannon and Anthony Stewart exemplify differing interpretive communities through their respective readings of Everett's novel, *Suder* (1983). Placed back-to-back in *Perspectives on Percival Everett*, the two essays simultaneously remind readers of the limited scholarship on Everett, particularly regarding this first novel and the complexity of Everett's work where two highly individualized readings occur. In "A Bird of a Different Feather: Blues, Jazz, and the Difficult Journey to the Self in Percival Everett's *Suder*," Cannon writes of Everett's movement through the blues and jazz aesthetics as a means of African Americans moving from being defined to having experienced the freedom of defining themselves, while Stewart uses his essay, "'Do you mind if we make Craig Suder white?': From Stereotype to Cosmopolitan to Grotesque in Percival Everett's *Suder*," to argue that the protagonist, Craig Suder, employs the grotesque in order to release himself from the burdens of universal representations of the black experience.

Though scholarship on Everett has been limited thus far, and what has been produced has primarily focused on his works of fiction, Sarah Wyman provides a thoughtful and theoretical analysis of Everett's latest collection of poetry, *re: f (gesture)* (2006). "Charting the Body: Percival Everett's Corporeal Landscapes in *re: f (gesture)*" emphasizes the author's interest in the body witnessed in both written and visual form, and resumes the structuralist critique of Everett's work found earlier within this collection noting the relationship between the concept of the sign and its representation. Doing so, Wyman situates Everett within a broader collective of writers and theorists than heretofore understood.

Editor and contributor Robin G. Vander concludes *Perspectives on Percival Everett* with a performance-based reading of Everett's retelling of the Greek tragedy, *Medea*. In "When the Text Becomes the Stage: Percival Everett's Performance Turn in *For Her Dark Skin*," Vander explores Everett's enlistment of performance writing praxis for developing the narrative. As with many of the essays throughout the collection, Vander's concluding essay connects with earlier contributors' reflections on the performative aspect of Everett's work including those provided by Dittman and Wyman.

Inarguably, it is impossible for any one source to exhaust the possibilities for reading and interpreting the meanings and significance of the writings of Percival Everett. It is our collective hope that here, within these pages, these essays help to illuminate the breadth and intellectual depth of Percival Everett's published works and will inspire established and emerging scholars to begin reading his works or to renew their interests—deservedly. Scholar, novelist, essayist, poet, artist. Accomplished and prolific—Percival Everett. To be continued.

PERSPECTIVES ON
PERCIVAL EVERETT

Chapter 1

"knowledge^2 + certainty^2 = squat^2"

(re)Thinking Identity and Meaning in Percival Everett's
The Water Cure

JONATHAN DITTMAN

Many of Percival Everett's works question how identities and perceptions of reality are created in society and expose the inherent flaws that exist within these systems of understanding. For example, in *Erasure* (2001), Everett's most critically acclaimed novel, Thelonius Monk Ellison wrestles with the need to "prove [he] was black enough" when describing a review that criticizes his retelling of Aeschylus' *The Persians* because it "has [nothing] to do with the African American experience" (2). In *The Water Cure* (2007), Everett continues this discussion of meaning and identity within the narrative of Ishmael Kidder, a man whose daughter is raped and murdered. Everett uses this narrative to frame his argument on how people do not exist with a preestablished identity or definition, but are represented through visual and linguistic signs that create specific meanings within a culture. Everett also demonstrates how these ideologies can be confronted or altered through the language used to define them, thereby changing the interpretations that had previously existed. The relationship between identification and meaning not only applies within the narrative of Ishmael Kidder, but also in the larger context of Percival Everett's own construction of racial and authorial identity; while he is racially identified by society as an "African American writer," he chooses for himself to exist as a "writer" who happens to be African American. How are we to understand the "African American" literary tradition when writers like Everett challenge our very conceptions of what that actually means?[1] What is the criterion for a work to be considered "African American" and must it represent "the black experience" to be considered as such? As a result of this uncertainty, all notions of identity and meaning become displaced through the language Everett uses to construct it and new interpretations of truth (or perceptions of truth) derive from within this framework.

In an interview with Anthony Stewart, Percival Everett is described as "An African American who does not presume to write about 'the African American experience'" (293), a signification furthered by Everett, who states, "I can't represent African-Americans. No one can" (303). In explicating the distinction between projection and perception, Everett claims that works written by African Americans are not required to differ in terms of genre or content from any other collection of writers:

> the failing is not in what we [African American writers] show but in how it is seen. And it is not just white readers, but African-American readers as well who seek to fit our stories to an existent model. It is not seeing with "white" eyes, it is seeing with "American" eyes, with brainwashed, automatic, comfortable, and "safe" perceptions of reality. ("Signing" 10)

The disruption of these preexisting conceptions is a major focal point in *The Water Cure*, emerging from both within Kidder's narrative and also through the system of identification in Everett's broader discourse on linguistic meaning. Paralleling a discourse that explores how "most language users have not been educated to identify ideologies, but rather to read texts as natural, inevitable representations of reality," Everett examines the way that these cultural assumptions define meaning (Eggins 11). What is seen, or perceived, by society is not necessarily a result of authorial intention but rather a product of adhering to ideologies that are embedded in our systems of understanding; systems rooted in the past as well as in present cultural contexts. In *The Water Cure*, Kidder's name allegorically represents the protagonist's tendency to play with language, and it is significant to Everett's point since it alludes to the unstable and perhaps inaccurate portrayal of his narrative, reconfiguring the ways in which texts are read, and diverging from the "comfortable" or "safe" approach referred to above.

Everett explores the assertion that readers are trained with certain preexisting frames of reference by stating: "It's not a bad thing. It's just a thing. This is the culture in which we live . . . It's not a good thing. It's not a bad thing. But it's a thing. But it doesn't mean it has to remain that way" (Stewart 300). It is this reconfiguration of social identities that encompasses a large portion of Everett's works, though in *The Water Cure*, Everett attacks these cultural assumptions through the language that created them. For instance, within Kidder's narrative, Everett repetitiously rearranges or displaces standard English with seemingly incongruent or indiscernible lexis: "Nyet, I cuncider this life a prism, meself mhad, tall this in spite of my comforit, sew-called, exstream combfort that costs me so much discomfjord and then gilt for feeling bad abut feeling good and one tit goes untilt the doctorn enters the asshighlum" (*Water* 16). Everett's unconventional use of lexical construction therefore results in an act of "defamiliarization," a concept pioneered by Russian formalist Viktor Shklovsky, which asserts that "The purpose of art is to impart the sensation of things as they are perceived and not as they are known" and that through this act of defamiliarization, objects are "made unfamiliar both by the description and by the proposal to change its form without changing its nature" ("Art" 16). Therefore, when Everett presents the reader with the sentence, "Nyet, I cuncider this life a prism," he is reconstructing the typical approach of writing, "And yet, I consider this life a prison," in order to address how language acts as a tool that can rework our perception of the world around us, an idea reminiscent of Shklovsky's claim that "After we see an object several times, we begin to recognize it. The object is in front of us and we know about it, but we do not see it—hence we cannot say anything significant about it" (16). By reconfiguring the standard production of English prose, Everett forces the reader to slow down and reexamine atypical visualizations of language if they are to discern any sense of meaning from the sentences. Therefore, what was initially seen and perceived as nonsensical, or undecipherable text, is actually meaningful if reexamined and unpacked from its current construction.

Everett's concern with the assumption that meaning is fixed or absolute is addressed most clearly through Kidder's inclusion of Plato's "allegory of the cave":

Plato: So, you get the picture of the cave and big fire?
Glaucon: I do.
Plato: And you can see the men walking by, carrying things?
Glaucon: I do.

Plato: Can you see that they see only their shadows on the wall?
Glaucon: I do.
Plato: And if they were to talk, wouldn't they name the things before them?
Glaucon: They would.
Plato: But remember that all they see is shadows, and further suppose that an echo circles around them, comes from the other side of the camp, and that they cannot see where it comes from, that in fact they hear only the echo and not the voice, and really, I want you to imagine now that all these men see is the mere shadows of images and nothing at all more, and I want you to tell me just what it is then that they are naming. (*Water* 210–11)

In this instance, Everett draws on Plato's allegory to illustrate how unstable perceptions of truth can be in society. The shadows of the images cast upon the cave wall are metaphorically tied to the notion that language, or the visual representations of language, is ephemeral and lacks absolute signification. Michel Foucault addresses this idea of meaning and representation in his analysis of Magritte's drawing *"Ceci n'est pas une pipe"* ("This Is Not a Pipe") by examining how we often conflate these two concepts (meaning and representation) as one—stating that one must "dissociate carefully . . . a representation from what it represents," taking all of the resultant conclusions on what a something represents, and then "multiply by two" (2: 188). Whereas language requires a consensual agreement between speaker/hearer and writer/reader in order to make sense, perceptions, as Everett clarifies through Plato's allegory, exist as a tenuous connection between images and names: "For Plato, the sense of it becomes that things *are* true when they are perceived, and that the perceptions of individuals are equally true" (*Water* 95). If the individual within the cave is looking at and identifying the objects based on the shadows alone, he is not necessarily providing the "correct" name to correlate with the image, that is, the name society has deemed as correctly identifying the object.

The idea that these cultural assumptions are often falsely perceived or surrounded by inaccurate categorizations, however, is addressed by the linguist Suzanne Eggins, who states:

> Since most of the lexical systems we use exist prior to us, we are often not conscious of the conventions on which they depend. As we tend to see language as a natural, naming device, it becomes difficult for us to think about dimensions of reality other than those which are encoded for us in our linguistic systems . . . semiotic theory demonstrates that the world is not out there as some absolute, determined reality simply to be labelled [*sic*] (and therefore talked about) in only one possible way. (18)

Hence, before an individual even enters into these codifications of meaning, a standardization of lexical interpretation has already been formed and accepted by a majority of the culture. The inclusion of African American readers in such constructions is highlighted by Everett when he cites that "African-Americans [fall] as much victim to culture as anyone else, learning the same ways, reading the same, predictable ways, and wanting to read the same, predictable literature" ("Foreword" xvi). The difficulty Everett stresses lies in questioning and ultimately diverging from systems that no longer represent the current culture. Everett's observation is therefore not limited to a specific race or classification of people; these assumptions are oftentimes fixed and can be performed by all cognitive beings.

In *The Water Cure*, Everett portrays this notion of instability by having the protagonist internally debate the meaning behind his actions toward the man believed to have raped and murdered his daughter. Kidder imprisons the accused and proceeds to torture him using a method referred to as "waterboarding," or "The Water Cure," in which the victim experiences a simulation of drowning. In response to the rhetorical question put forth in his text ("Did you" commit these acts of torture?), Kidder announces:

> [I]t all comes back to that indifference to the marked thing, the way nouns and names behave badly and play loose with meaning, the

way language resists the tightening of the screws and the sketching of schema . . . the whole mess of language yearning for a decent visual metaphor to connect it with the world toward which it is so indifferent. The true answer to your question is shorter than the lie. Did you? I did. (*Water* 7)

Kidder's simple, truthful admission, "I did," comes after significant qualifications and justifications for his actions against the man who may or may not be responsible for his daughter's death. In terms of the "visual metaphor," or Saussure's "sound-image," Kidder's rationalization that he is "merely a sign, a clear sign, and like any sign . . . indifferent to the nature of the thing that [he] designate[s]," is a prime example of how arbitrary symbols can be in the construction of meaning (*Water* 7). For Saussure, the importance or implication of a sign is derived from its relation to other signs and is collectively agreed upon (Eggins 190). Through Kidder's existence as an "indifferent" sign we are able to see his opposition to the conscientious nature of truth he avoids through his complex wordplay. As a result, the statement, "I did," becomes more representational of truth for Kidder than his carefully constructed lie.

With Kidder's confession defined in these terms, Everett has expounded upon his previous observation in *Erasure*: "It's incredible that a sentence is ever understood. Mere sound strung together by some agent attempting to mean some thing, but the meaning need not and does not confine itself to that intention" (44). Language does not adhere to a set framework of understanding (or schema), but rather it becomes a sort of organic entity that adapts to the world around it—a world in which, according to Kidder, language is indifferent. Everett describes language in *The Water Cure* as a sort of "disposable ladder, one that once we achieve our level of meaning we kick away and wonder how we got to where we are," and reaffirms the mercurial nature of linguistic meaning through Kidder's declaration: "I am not interested in what meaning you will make when reading the words on these pages, if you choose or can make any meaning at all, but in the *limits* of what meaning you can make" (36–37, 49, my emphasis). Kidder is therefore not concerned with any attempts at providing finite or conclusive interpretations, but with the innumerable possibilities or meanings one can derive through language.

The idea that language fluctuates and exists outside a set structure is furthered by Everett through a discussion on the functional aspects of framing. Specifically, this observation focuses on how certain lenses or constraints are deemed necessary for understanding. As Kidder explicates in one of his narratorial breaks:

> It is always a matter of framing, of framing matter. Of paintings, whether they are framed or not, whether the frame wears the work or whether the frame is an essential part of some artistic expression . . . And after all a frame is just a box, and a box is just a container, but what a container does, in addition to *containing*, if it ever does that at all, marking what is inside, is mark what is outside. A box, a frame, a container, one's skin not so much surround a thing, but close out a world that is not surrounded. (*Water* 7)

In this instance, if a box, frame, or one's skin serves to illustrate that it is nothing more than a sort of container, or vessel, then how are we to perceive what the frame *actually* represents? The answer lies not in what the box contains, but in the way it is received externally by those observing it. In terms of race, one's skin acts as a "visual metaphor" though at any time this rudimentary notion of labeling may be incompatible with what is unseen, a notion Ishmael Kidder further explicates by stating:

> We're always about the business of *what* a thing means. I want to know *why* a thing means . . . there are three layers of bullshit that we must penetrate—and then a fourth and a fifth (afterthoughts). They are, first, a name; second, a description; third, an image; fourth and fifth, the knowledge of the thing and the thing itself. Afterthoughts. And what about the reality of the *image*? (*Water* 145, my italics)

Kimberly Eaton, in her discussion of *Erasure* explains how language cannot necessarily convey "consistent meaning . . . because the linguistic message receiver will interpret based on their own understanding instead of that of the sender's" (221). As a result of this linguistic fluidity, representations through language are largely subjective since, as Eaton points out, the message being sent can be altered by those perceiving it. Kidder's differentiation between *"what* a thing means" and *"why* a thing means" addresses the problematic nature of identification. Since it's been established that meaning can fluctuate or prove inconsistent, an interpretation or identification of *what* a thing represents is ever changing, potentially harboring the "layers of bullshit" that comprise Kidder's confession. If the reality of something is based on three identifiers—"name," "description," and the "image"—there would never be an instance in which meaning could deviate from its conventional application. The question of *"why* a thing means," however, is fundamentally complicated, if not impossible, to discern in the same manner. By asking "why" a thing means what it does, Everett is able to confront and challenge the preexisting conventions of identity and meaning that are often times followed blindly by society and reaffirm his statement that "$knowledge^2 + certainty^2 = squat^2$" (*Water* 96).

Everett's stance on diffusing these presuppositions about identity is reflected most significantly in *The Water Cure* through Kidder's appropriation of a female pseudonym for the publication of his romance novels, in which he explains: "Initially, I adopted a pseudonymous existence both as a means and as an end. A black man wasn't going to sell many romance novels to school middle-aged perm-headed nail-decaled bus drivers, beauticians, and trailer parkers" (202–3). Kidder's declaration is significant in two ways: (1) the writer's assumption of *who would read* these types of novels; (2) the reader's assumption of *who would write* these novels. According to Everett, "African-American writers were, and in some ways still are, stuck trying to supply fictions that are palatable to American culture's tastes and expectations and do not upset the way America wants to see black people and itself" ("Foreword" xvi). As a result, Kidder dualistically represents how society constructs identities and how individuals can deflate these systems of understanding; not only is Kidder producing works that readers would not associate with an African American, but also what readers would not expect from a man.

Likewise, in *Erasure*, Everett has his protagonist, Monk Ellison, assume the "Bad Man" or "Bad Nigger" persona of Stagg R. Leigh in order to subvert cultural assumptions of a writer needing to portray the "black experience" in order to produce "authentic" African American literature[2]

(Deutsch 67). In Monk Ellison's novella, *My Pafology*, the protagonist, Van Go Jenkins, is also characterized as the "Bad Nigger," typified by gang violence and ill treatment of women, and socially marked by his use of inner-city dialect. Monk ponders this perception of identity through language most clearly when he states:

> The pain started in my feet and coursed through my legs, up my spine and into my brain and I remembered passages of *Native Son* and *The Color Purple* and *Amos and Andy* . . . people in the street shouting *dint*, *ax*, *fo*, *screet* and *fahvre!* and I was screaming inside, complaining that I didn't sound like that, that my mother didn't sound like that, that my father didn't sound like that and I imagined myself sitting on a park bench . . . and a man came up to me and he asked me what I was doing and my mouth opened and I couldn't help what came out, "Why fo you be axin?" (*Erasure* 61–62)

What Monk is suggesting in his criticism of presumptive identities is not the absence of black Americans who use language in this manner—for certainly African American Vernacular English (AAVE) is an acceptable mode of communication within communities—but rather that linguistic signifiers, in this case dialectical signification, cannot form a concrete or fixed identity. What the "black experience" is for some is not universal or characteristic of an essentialist or "collective" belief. In addition, the use of "code-switching" further displaces to the fixed notion of identity since it enables the user to change from one dialect, or speech pattern, to another (Lippi-Green 43). For example, while Monk speaks and writes in Standard American English, his fictitious persona, Stagg R. Leigh, employs the use of AAVE in both oral and written modes—a performance that is deemed by society as more "genuinely" black than Monk's.

Though Monk's intention for his novella (a mockery of "true" black experience, originally titled *My Pafology*, later published as *Fuck*) is to be a scathing satire of the publishing industry and societal beliefs, it is ironically misunderstood and receives the Book Award in fiction for its authentic representation of African American culture. The Book Award committee reads, or sees, a different text than the one Ellison intended:

"I learned a lot reading that book," John Paul Sigmarsen said. "I haven't had a lot of experience with color—black people—and so *Fuck* was a great thing for me." "That's exactly what I'm talking about," I said. "People will read this shit and believe that there is truth to it."

Thomas Tomad laughed. "This is the truest novel I've ever read . . . It's the real thing." (*Erasure* 261)

The ubiquitous paradox surrounding Sigmarsen and Tomad's comments is quite apparent when read in conjunction with Monk's earlier discourse regarding "*dint, ax, fo, screet* and *fahvre*" (*Erasure* 61). While there certainly are members of the African American community that speak within this linguistic system, it cannot be understood as universal or an accurate representation of "the real thing," that is, genuine "black experience." The irony, therefore, is that since Monk and Stagg are actually the same person, this act of code-switching allows Monk to literally shift identities and further disrupt the committee's conception of truth. However, the difficulty of adhering to one belief or the other ultimately distorts Monk's own sense of which identity is "authentic," ending with the hard-laced, imposing figure of Stagg R. Leigh conflating his persona by looking into the TV cameras and saying, "Egads, I'm on television" (*Erasure* 265). In this moment Ellison's linguistic choice, "Egads," contradicts the vernacular and visual representation of the "Bad Man" expected by those attending the Book Award ceremony. As a result, we see what E. Patrick Johnson refers to as an instance in which an individual's "authenticity is called into question . . . not solely on phenotype but also on the symbolic relationship between skin color and the performance of culturally inscribed language or dialect that refers back to an 'essential' blackness or whiteness" (*Appropriating Blackness* 5–6). Therefore, not only has the committee overlooked Ellison's satirical intention of *Fuck*, but Monk's own physical, vocal, and experiential identity has also been misconstrued.

In *The Water Cure*, the introduction of Kidder's feminine alter ego and artistic pseudonym, Estelle Gilliam, also deconstructs identity in relation to existing American ideologies about gender. Kidder's use of a female persona results in the culture questioning his masculinity. When Kidder first moves to a remote house in the town of Taos, New Mexico, he makes the assertion: "I simply am of course who I am, Ishmael Kidder, but I am better known as Estelle Gilliam, the romance novelist. No one knows that I am Estelle Gilliam, not around here" (*Water* 25). However, moments later Kidder acknowledges to the reader that "The local constable knows; I was forced to confess my identity to forestall his presumption that I was, in his words, 'a drug runnin' bastard dog son of a bitch'" (25). Kidder's declaration to the constable that he earns his living through a female persona can be found as particularly emasculating in American society. Later, when the sheriff suggests that Kidder should shoot the drug dealers who are diverting Kidder's water supply, he responds:

Me: Bucky, it sounds to me as if you're encouraging me to break a few laws.

Sheriff: There's the law and there's the law. There might be a law against it, but that doesn't mean you can't do it. The law is just words after all.

Me: That scares me.

Sheriff: It should. It's the American way. (*Water* 118)

In order to reclaim the masculinity lost in his admission to the sheriff about his feminine identity, Kidder goes along with the sheriff's suggestion and waits for the drug dealers in the woods. In order to defend his masculine identity, Kidder must conform to the "American way" alluded to by the sheriff.[3] As a result of this challenge, Kidder plays into the conventional assumption that masculinity equals violence:

My shotgun is old, a Winchester Model 12 with ventilated rib . . . It is loaded, here in the dark, no moon, only sneaking sounds in the brush below me, with one and one-eight loads of number 8 shot, each containing 460 pellets. It is a cold weapon, but each time I lift it, I feel so, so, so American, with my full choke bore and so many chances to miss and so much potential to do harm, so American, I might fire into the night just to see the flash of the barrel, to have my ears ring . . . and kill something, someone, something. (*Water* 193)

Kidder's statements about guns and killing are diametrically opposed from the thematic elements of Gilliam's romance novels. Whereas Gilliam's world is populated with works such as *The Wind's Kiss* and *The Recovery of Passion*, Kidder desires for the next novel to involve the "story of Lucien Raines, a young painter making his ruthless way in New York society and of his sponsor Davida Hume and the love they deny and finally find only to have it cause so much pain for them and all those around them that they end it all in a suicide pact" (*Water* 67). Therefore, when Kidder is about to leave the hills without shooting the drug dealers, he diverges from the feminine embodiment of Estelle and embraces the violent aspect of his "masculine" identity, citing: "The floodgates of rage and anger and justice and the AMERICAN WAY open . . . So, bang bang away. Bang" (194). Violence toward others, while antithetical to Estelle Gilliam, becomes a necessary tool for Kidder's reclamation of the masculine identity lost through his appropriation of a feminine alter ego.

The motif of diametrically opposed identities (Monk/Van Go; Ishmael/Estelle) in Everett's novels points to the discourse surrounding authorial intent, existence, and function theorized by Roland Barthes and Michel Foucault. In "The Death of the Author," Barthes posits that "writing is the destruction of every voice, every origin . . . where all identity is lost, beginning with the very identity of the body that writes" (49). This particular statement is highly reflective in Everett's representation of the writers in his novels for the dichotomy of how the author and his pseudonym are expected to be *seen* or understood is ever present. In both *Erasure* and *The Water Cure*, the protagonists are unable to reconcile which self is more authentic or accurate and in essence are destroyed in the manner Barthes refers to. Barthes's inclusion of the actual author or "*scriptor*" of the work in this loss also harkens back to Everett's statements about his inability to *truly* represent African Americans through his writing (53). Likewise, Foucault's statements about authorial function indicate that it "does not refer purely and simply to a real individual, since it can give rise simultaneously to several selves, to several subjects—positions that can be occupied by different classes of individuals" ("Author" 2: 216). Therefore, what *Erasure* and *The Water Cure* illustrate most pointedly is a struggle between what an author's function is (from both Everett's fictionalized perspectives and his own) and what the publishing industry or society as a whole believes an author should be. As with Barthes's "Death of an Author," the layering of identities or selves in Everett's works denotes construction, and deconstruction, of a multitude of voices—each representing a different reality.

Similarly, Kidder also disrupts the notion of identity formation through the performative acts of naming. As mentioned above, Kidder's identity performance largely included the creation of a feminine pseudonym, Estelle Gilliam. However, the act of naming is important not only for the disruption of Kidder's own identity, but also for the eradication of his victim's own existence. During his interrogation of the man believed to have murdered his daughter, Kidder plays with the concept of names as identifying markers and how this notion can be destabilized or altered on a whim:

> "Do you have a name?"
>
> "Yes."
>
> "Don't tell me. Names are always just substitutes for nouns, and you know what good nouns are. I will name you. I'll do that for you. The performative act of name will be yet another little thing I do to you. I name you W. Poor, poor W. 'Where is W?' they are asking. 'Who cares?' others are saying . . . But I'd rather have you consider that I have renamed you Art and now you are Art and no longer W. My God, what have I done to you? Poor, poor W. now has a new name. Just like that, a new name." (*Water* 91)

Just as Saussure's "signified" was arbitrarily represented by a sound-image, or "signifier," so is Kidder's construction of his victim's name. In Kidder's demonstration, the name "W." is as indifferent to the object being represented as "Art" is; neither signification represents any essential meaning, it is only through language that any meaning is constructed. But, as Kidder points out, the meaning presented in this instance is as tenuous and unstable as the names that signify them—both are subject to revision and cannot concretely identify an object.

In light of this revelation, Kidder asks his bound victim, Art (or perhaps W.), "What is a stable identity?" (*Water* 126). Kidder answers this rhetorical question by stating:

> You are not the man you were when we met, not the same man you were before I tied you up to that plank. You are not the same man who

raped and murdered my little girl. Even though you are, you are not. You were the sinner, but now you are the punished, someone new altogether. The question is, are you the same man? . . . You have all new skin and hair from when you were a child, your blood is new, the cells that make up your organs have been replaced, but you're still you, aren't you? Maybe it all comes back to names, but people change their names, get called different things, forget their names. So, it's not how you appear and it's not what you're made of and it's not what you're called. So, what is it? I'll tell you what I think, I think that we never change. (*Water* 126–27)

Through Kidder's observation we are able to see how fragile conceptions of identity really are. None of the tools used to construct or reflect identities in society can remain fixed; lexical and sociological systems are always changing. In Kidder's example, names are unstable and cannot denote a comprehensive or holistic identity. While categorically significant linguistic markers, such as husband, father, and son, can refer to the same individual, these markers cannot independently define a person—more comprehensive qualifiers are necessary to even scratch the surface of identity. Essentially, the importance Everett draws attention to in this passage is that while there is an underlying and perhaps "genuine" description of an individual, the layers of meaning encoded in all of these symbolic representations make it impossible to truly identify a person.

Throughout *The Water Cure*, Everett repeatedly illustrates how conceptions of truth are disrupted by the very nature of language. At the forefront of Everett's discussion is how these linguistic systems of representation can be altered or amended to form new meanings in society. Everett uses Kidder as a figure who destabilizes our perceptions of the world in order to fully illustrate how questionable the notion of "absolute truth" really is. The condensed narrative surrounding Ishmael Kidder and his action toward a man *he* names "Art" serves as the framework for the larger, metadiscourse Everett supplies for the reader. This discussion incorporates all aspects of identity that are accepted as fixed by individuals. Similarly, the visual signifiers used to denote Percival Everett as an African American writer (primarily skin color) presents us with a limited discussion of what Everett's writing represents. Furthermore, it calls into question the whole notion of "black experience" as a requirement for "black authenticity." With writers such as Everett diverging from the thematic elements of Richard Wright's *Native* Son (the work parodied in *My Pafology*), and Ralph Ellison's *Invisible Man*, there is a definite need to rethink what constitutes the African American literary tradition. For as Everett exposes in *The Water Cure*, language, the vehicle used to convey meaning in culture, is anything but stable.

Notes

1. It should also be noted, that while Percival Everett deals with this topic throughout his works, numerous African American writers have addressed this same issue. According to Keith Mitchell and Robin Vander, "Charles Chesnutt (*Evelyn's Husband* and *A Business Career*), Richard Wright (*Savage Holiday*), James Baldwin (*Giovanni's Room*) . . . all wrote novels in which the protagonists were white." Likewise, aside from Baldwin's *Giovanni's Room*, which "was not initially well-received by black critics and is not viewed as an 'African American' novel, per se . . . [these works] have rarely been seriously critically examined by either black or white scholars."

2. According to James I. Deutsch, "The Bad Man is a recurring figure in African American folklore, representing the rebellious character of those black men who refuse to submit to authority and may use violence to achieve their ends" (67). In this case, Monk chooses to go by the name Stagg R. Leigh, an obvious parallel to Stagolee, who, as Deutsch points out, is a "folkloric figure . . . who turns upon everyone in their way, whether black or white, usually with amoral violence" (67). For further reading on this figure, see Cecil Brown, *Stagolee Shot Billy* (Cambridge: Harvard University Press, 2003), or the graphic novel by Derek McCulloch and Shepherd Hendrix, *Stagger Lee* (Berkeley: Image Comics, 2006).

3. Furthermore, the mercurial nature of language is highlighted in *The Water Cure* through Kidder's scathing condemnation of the Bush administration's interrogation techniques, legislature (such as the Patriot Act), and the manipulation of the media in order to convey a false sense of truth and reality. In naming the work *The Water Cure*, Everett is exposing the deceitful way language was used by the Central Intelligence Agency to justify their actions for torturing suspects by simulating drowning in a technique referred to as "waterboarding" or "The Water Cure." Defenders of this interrogation technique have communicated its effective use in protecting America, whereas opponents claim this to be illegal, citing the prosecution

of Japanese interrogators after World War II for the same practices. For further press accounts, see Scott Shane, "Waterboarding Used 266 Times on 2 Suspects," *New York Times on the Web*, April 20, 2009. http://www.nytimes.com/2009/04/20/world/20detain.html (accessed August 3, 2009); Mark Mazzetti and Scott Shane, "Interrogation Memos Detail Harsh Tactics by the C.I.A," *New York Times on the Web*, April 17, 2009. http://www.nytimes.com/2009/04/17/us/politics/17detain.html (accessed August 3, 2009); and David Stout, "Holder Tells Senators Waterboarding is Torture," *New York Times on the Web*, January 16, 2009. http://www.nytimes.com/2009/01/16/us/politics/16holdercnd.html (accessed August 3, 2009).

Chapter 2

"This Strange Juggler's Game"

Forclusion in Percival Everett's I Am Not Sidney Poitier

SARAH MANTILLA GRIFFIN

The naming has done either the damage or the work and cannot be undone. The naming has created the thing itself and then to go look for that which makes it that thing is to fail to acknowledge that in the first place its existence must be verified; having been named not constituting the same as really being (REF. unicorn). —PERCIVAL EVERETT, *ERASURE* (2001)

In his short 1991 treatise, "Signing to the Blind," Percival Everett recounts his experience with Embassy Pictures as they sought to turn his novel *Suder* (1983) into a motion picture. "Norman Lear's army," he states, turned down Sidney Poitier as supporting actor and director of the film because "he was not a good enough director" (10). On the contrary, Everett continues, "If anyone in Hollywood could have done the story correctly, understood it, it was Sidney Poitier" (10). Sidney Poitier, the first black man to win an Academy Award for Best Actor, is famous for his politically charged work both on- and off-screen, and for his ability to remain nonetheless accepted by mainstream audiences. Poitier consciously defied stereotypes through his portrayals of a variety of characters; he stated in a 2008 interview with Larry King that control over the characters he played was important to him because: "I had a sense of responsibility not only to myself and to my time, but certainly to the people I represented" ("Interview with Sidney Poitier"). This understanding of the people he "represented" is what Poitier would have brought to *Suder*, and is what his name brings

19

to Everett's latest novel, *I Am Not Sidney Poitier* (2009). Of the choice to use Poitier in this work, Everett has said: "I was interested in the icon of the palatable black man in the '60s or '70s" (Toal). Poitier as icon, or symbol, is central to *I Am Not Sidney Poitier*, which joins the conversation about symbols and signification that pervades Everett's work.

As Margaret Russett and others have discussed, Everett's interest in signification is quite clear in his 2001 novel, *Erasure*. At an academic conference, the novel's protagonist, Thelonious Monk Ellison, presents a semiotic analysis of Roland Barthes's *S/Z* (1970), which is a structuralist analysis of Honoré de Balzac's famous short story "Sarrasine" (1850). Of *S/Z*, Monk writes:

> *The S/Z refers no doubt to the unvoiced and voiced, but the enigma pales in consideration of the slash which separates them. The "/" at once combines S and the Z into the title/anti-title, and divides them . . . The "/" is also that line which we have come to accept as the greasy and shifting mark, however dimensionless, between the signifier and the signified.* (original emphasis, 14)

This "greasy and shifting mark" is that with which Everett is most interested; *I Am Not Sidney Poitier* offers a new entree into the question of the line between signifier and signified by rethinking one of *Erasure*'s central issues, that of negation. Everett explores negation and its relationship to subjective doubling in *Erasure* through Monk's creation of Stagg R. Leigh, an alter ego that he is forced to inhabit, to the possible destruction of his original self. Erasure and doubling again take center stage in *I Am Not Sidney Poitier*; however, the erasure in this novel is of a primordial nature best explained through Jacques Lacan's conception of *forclusion*, or foreclosure.[1] Although related, forclusion departs from negation, as defined by Sigmund Freud and others,[2] in that it refers to an originary exclusion of a signifier; the signifier is not repressed, but is rejected completely from the signifying field before one is aware of it. According to Lacan, this rejection sets the stage for a return of the excluded not in the symbolic realm, as in the return of the repressed, but instead in the real, in the form of hallucination. The signifier in question is what Lacan calls the primordial signifier, a "pure" signifier, detached from meaning, which must be acknowledged as such in order for one to become a subject. Forclusion necessitates

a consideration of the power of language to create subjects and their realities; while *I Am Not Sidney Poitier* is, like Everett's other novels, a challenging of identity categories, it is first and foremost a meditation on language
and subjectivity.

Everett places Lacan's ideas into the most unlikely of situations; the
subject of forclusion and thus the victim of the "strange juggler's game"
in *I Am Not Sidney Poitier* is a young black man named Not Sidney Poitier.
Not Sidney is "filthy, obscenely, uncomfortably rich" due to his mother's
investment in the Turner Broadcasting System (6). "Born after two years
of hysterical gestation," Not Sidney is marked by strangeness even before
he is born (3).[3] Not Sidney notes of himself:

> I flew with confusion always parallel to me, and a whole internal chase
> at my rear. The one matter that was not confusing to me, but seemed
> to escape all others, was the fact that the only thing that was certain
> to become obsolete, would necessarily become wearied and worn, was
> the truth. I knew this in spite of the *truth* that I had had little truck with
> *truth* in my life. It was not that I considered myself a resident in a den of
> lies, but rather that my history was shrouded and diced and soaking wet
> with hysteria and contradiction. (original emphasis, 29)

Not Sidney's missing truth serves to answer Lacan's question about just
that topic; specifically, in his 1955–1956 seminar, "The Psychoses," Lacan
asks: "What happens when the truth of the thing is lacking . . . when for
example the register of the father defaults . . . What happens if a certain
lack occurs in the formative function of the father?" (204). These questions are significant in answering Lacan's main question, namely: "How
does one enter psychosis?" (157). Lacan argues that there are three orders
of the psyche: the symbolic, the imaginary, and the real, and that the
"strange juggler's game" among these orders defines human relationships
with reality (Lacan 47). *I Am Not Sidney Poitier* enters this juggler's game,
presenting both a parody of and a reply to the questions posed in Lacan's
seminar and, more importantly, to questions of Not Sidney's being. By
accepting the implications of Lacan's arguments—even those Lacan dis-
missed—and letting Lacan's ideas play out to their logical ends, Everett
allows the ideas to parody themselves, to agree with themselves, and to

suggest alternative formulations. Thus, although Lacan states: "I in no way believe that there is anywhere at all a moment, a stage, at which the subject first acquires the primitive signifier, that subsequently the play of meanings is introduced, and that after that, signifier and signified having linked arms, we then enter the domain of discourse. All the same, there is a representation here that is so indispensable that I feel comfortable about giving it to you" (151). Everett focuses solely on this representation and employs it in I Am Not Sidney Poitier, embodying Lacan's ideas in just the way that Lacan did not necessarily intend.

Not Sidney grows up to bear a striking resemblance to the actor and director Sidney Poitier, a coincidence that he thinks: "my poor disturbed and now deceased mother could not have known when I was born" (3). In fact, Not Sidney notes that his mother did not name him with Sidney Poitier in mind: "my name had nothing to do with the actor at all . . . *Not Sidney* was simply a name she had created, with no consideration of the outside world" (7). This handsome, rich black man with a strange name, who owns much of one of the largest media companies in the world, is the subject through which Everett explores Lacan's conception of forclusion. Based as forclusion is on the multiplicity of meanings possible in relation to any signifier, this complexly signifying subject is fertile ground for a consideration of forclusion's theoretical possibilities. Moreover, in documenting this play of signifiers within such a broad signifying field, the novel adds to Lacan's questions: What is the most important signifier in the construction of Not Sidney's subjectivity? This question is vital to Everett's project in this novel and elsewhere, as its answer demonstrates why the expected essential signifier in black writing—namely, race, or blackness—should not and cannot rightly be assumed to be the dominant signifier, attached securely to a signified, in writing by and about black people (which many critics consistently take it for granted to be).

Lacan posits naming as a signifying practice that makes meaning possible. Not Sidney's name, however, makes meaning impossible through its self-annihilation. This annihilation is evident in people's confusion and disbelief at his pronouncement of his name, such that his "real name became a mystery to be solved by many" (Everett 29). Not Sidney's name cannot signify without speaking a hole, a lack, at the space of being. That is, Not Sidney can never say "I am," but must always say "I am Not."[4] Thus, the Abbott-and-Costello-type "Who's On First" moments that reviewers have found so humorous are not simply comic relief, but actually punctuating the moments in which Not Sidney fails to respond to interpellation with "I," the moments in which he is fundamentally dead:

> "What's your name?" a kid would ask.
> "Not Sidney," I would say.
> "Okay, then what is it?"
> "I told you. It's Not Sidney."
> "Ain't nobody called you Sidney."
> "No, it's Not Sidney." (13)

The kid, as all humans, says "you" to interpellate an other (Not Sidney) to respond with "I." But when Not Sidney lacks the signifier to respond with "I," the interpellation turns to "eternal interrogation" in which "the *thou* reappears indefinitely" (Lacan 305). These moments continually point to the divide between signifier and signified that defines Not Sidney's being, and to the exclusion of the primordial signifier.

The exclusion inherent in Not Sidney's name parallels the exclusion in his life of his father. For Lacan, the Name-of-the-Father is an essential signifier, a structuring force in the symbolic order. The subject must be able to access the signifier "father" at least for the phallus to be more than just an appearance, and at most to intervene in the imaginary. In the first case, the symbolic father—or the phallus—is necessary in relationships between mother and child where the father has been primordially excluded and therefore proceeding through the Oedipus complex was never a possibility. Without going through this process, Lacan argues, one never moves from the imaginary order to the symbolic order and is thus at risk of psychosis. Such is the case with Not Sidney; he explains:

> The best I can figure is that my mother was in fact hysterically pregnant and that in month fourteen or so of that pregnancy she somehow managed to find and utilize the sexual organs of my father (a term I of course use in the strictest zoological sense), who may or may not have been Sidney Poitier, and she actually did become pregnant, and so here I am.[5] (5)

Not Sidney's connection of the father and Sidney Poitier in the space of the unknown, the excluded, is significant in the subsequent revelation of Not Sidney's psychosis. Not Sidney does not know the part of himself that is his father genetically, and does not know his being through naming, so naming and father meet in the unknown space of the Name-of-the-Father, the excluded Other, the primordial signifier, and on some level Sidney Poitier is placed into this order of the father. This placement occurs throughout the novel; at one point, Not Sidney is asked if Sidney Poitier is his father. He immediately replies in the negative, but then thinks: "I answered quite definitely, but the fact of the matter is I was not quite definite; I did not know" (84). In this way, what is happening on a symbolic level with his name is also happening in the real with his father, such that name and father are combined in the space excluded from the symbolic order, a literalizing or embodying of the Name-of-the-Father.

Naming and the absent or unknown father have been central concerns in black writing since chattel slavery in the Americas began. Through the Middle Passage, slaves were robbed of their African names and given European names, including the surnames of their owners, such that the name became a marker of captivity. Orlando Patterson considers the changing of slaves' names to be the "second major feature of the ritual of enslavement," and notes that the importance of a name is in that a name is "the verbal sign of his whole identity, his being-in-the-world as a distinct person" (54). Hence, the changing of slaves' names was a way to destroy identity and dehumanize. Within slave systems, slaves' names could be changed at random; in his narrative of his enslavement, William Wells Brown recounts the changing of his name, of which he states, "at the time, I thought to be one of the most cruel acts that could be committed upon my rights . . . Though young I was old enough to place a high appreciation upon my name" (333). Thus, choosing one's own name became, for black Americans, a powerful way to declare oneself, both politically and metaphysically, a "distinct person." Naming has since been central to black self-definition and has become a defining feature of the black American literary tradition.[6]

As with naming, the trope of the absent father began under the system of chattel slavery in the Americas, which separated families, robbing children of their fathers through sale. Slave children also lost their fathers through rape; that is, many of the absent fathers in black writing are rumored to be white men, usually slave masters, who raped their slaves and denied their children. Of the absence of the father for slaves, Frederick Douglass wrote: "A person of some consequence here in the north, sometimes designated *father*, is literally abolished in slave law and slave practice" (28). The impossibility of knowing one's paternity thus became a defining feature of slavery, and a convention in black literature, upon which *I Am Not Sidney Poitier* signifies. Not Sidney's absent father and problematic name place the novel within a tradition of black American writing; Everett's use of these tropes in conjunction with Lacanian psychoanalysis, however, sheds a new light on their possible meanings. Everett demonstrates that naming and the father may signify very differently throughout the history of black writing, yet remain key signifiers. Thus, by demonstrating the divide between signifier and signified, Everett can take part in the black literary tradition, can utilize its signifiers, without coming to expected conclusions. Further, *I Am Not Sidney Poitier* suggests that black experience, and black literary conventions, may have much to say about psychoanalytic theory. The novel compels a reading of the theory through the fiction, rather than solely vice versa.

The primordial exclusion of the father in Not Sidney's name, and literally in his life, has necessarily unhinged signifier and signified for him. Of this predicament, Lacan states: "the subject will have to bear the weight of this real, primitive dispossession of the signifier and adopt compensation for it, at length, over the course of his life, through a series of purely conformist identifications with characters who will give him the feeling for what one has to do to be a man" (205). Not Sidney's encounters with potential father figures fail to remedy the exclusion of the father and thus fail to unite signified and signifier, or to allow Not Sidney to express his being. For example, Ted Turner, the founder of Turner Broadcasting, takes Not Sidney into his home after the death of Not Sidney's mother; however, he outright rejects the possibility of becoming a surrogate father for Not Sidney because "to Turner's credit he was not comfortable with the scenario of the rich do-gooding white man taking in the poor little black child" (Everett 8). In Not Sidney's case, he could never be the "poor little black child" given the fact that he is extremely wealthy, but Turner rejects surrogate fatherhood nonetheless. By rejecting surrogate fatherhood, he also rejects the opportunity to be Not Sidney's surrogate Other, through which Not Sidney could have potentially created his ego, based his subjectivity.

Not Sidney meets his second potential father figure in college, in the form of his professor, Percival Everett. By giving his character the same name as himself, Everett again reinforces the divide between signifier and signified, specifically as it applies to names. In discussing the novel, from this point forward, one must distinguish the character from the author by signifiers other than name. Not Sidney enrolls in Everett's class, entitled "The Philosophy of Nonsense," in which Everett proceeds to string together sentences of academic jargon that ultimately mean nothing. In doing so, he demonstrates the divide between signifier and meaning, that instability central to Not Sidney's being, and provides an apt parody of empty academic discourse. As Not Sidney questions him as to the meaning of his lecture, Everett pauses and says:

> "You know what I see when I look at you?"
> "No."
> "I see Sidney Poitier."
> "But . . ."
> "I know, I know, you're Not Sidney Poitier and also not Sidney Poitier, but in a strange way you are Sidney Poitier as much as you're anyone." (102)

Everett names Sidney Poitier as a part of Not Sidney's ego long before Not Sidney encounters himself as Sidney Poitier. Everett is not performing the function of the father, but rather continually emphasizing that Not Sidney's problem is "a question of the signifier" (Lacan 195). He makes the question of the signifier "Sidney Poitier," as it applies to Not Sidney's life, abundantly clear as he tells Not Sidney to be himself. When Not Sidney asks who else he would be, Everett wisely replies: "I don't know. You might decide all of a sudden that you're Sidney Poitier. You're not, you know. Though you do look alarmingly like him" (123). Everett (the character) opens the door for Not Sidney to encounter his Other by bringing the signifier "Sidney Poitier" into Not Sidney's symbolic field, at least partially detached from the signified actor, as well as by pointing to Not Sidney's potentially damaging identification with the actor due to his resemblance.

As Lacan argues, the onset of psychosis is marked by "the word of revelation, which opens up a new dimension and gives a feeling of ineffable understanding . . . and on the other hand the refrain, the same old song" (255). Everett's statement captures the newness of "Sidney Poitier" as signifier while retaining the refrain of Not Sidney's annihilating name.

Lacan argues that the question raised by the lack of a signifier "manifests itself through fringe phenomena in which the set of signifiers is brought into play" (205).[7] The novel again literalizes this idea, as Not Sidney proceeds to experience moments from various Sidney Poitier films: *Guess Who's Coming to Dinner* (1967), *The Defiant Ones* (1958), *Lilies of the Field* (1963), and *In the Heat of the Night* (1967). He finds himself at dinner with his girlfriend's parents who think his skin is too dark, in prison chained to a racist white inmate who, he notes, "looks a little like that old movie star, Tony Curtis," assisting a group of nuns, and finally investigating a murder (Everett 74). In each situation, the meanings of "Sidney Poitier" and "Not Sidney Poitier" change based on the signifying field. Sidney Poitier's movies are famous for boldly exploring race relations—tensions, conflicts, ambiguities, and commonalities. In exploring these relations, Poitier had to signify in many different ways in order to challenge the meanings attached to signifiers like blackness, criminality, wealth, education, and so forth. Through divorcing signifiers from meaning and henceforth changing meanings, Poitier's characters were often able to change understandings of those signifiers. Everett (the author) tests the limits of Sidney Poitier as signifier in Not Sidney's encounters, which both correspond to and change the signifying fields of Poitier's films. Most notably, by interchanging signifiers including and interfacing with blackness, Everett demonstrates that the "icon of the palatable black man" is a multifaceted, malleable signifier.

By amending the signifying terms of Poitier's films, Everett at once demonstrates the inessentiality of race—or blackness—as a signifier, and reconfirms race as a signifier informing the trajectory of each encounter. For instance, in Not Sidney's experience of *Guess Who's Coming to Dinner*, his girlfriend's parents are black, not white. This racial switch upends the cultural dynamic underpinning the film's portrayal of the parents' unhappiness with the skin color of their daughter's suitor. Rather than a conversation about interracial relations, it becomes about intraracial prejudices, but with the same result: the parents in both cases initially disapprove of the union due to skin color. The subsequent introduction of the same signifier as existed in the original film, socioeconomic class, ultimately demonstrates that blackness can be palatable, regardless of the race of the palette, if it is tempered by wealth. Even this conclusion is destabilized, however, as the signifying "rich black man" is jailed both in Poitier's *In the Heat of the Night* and in Not Sidney's arrest in Smuteye, Alabama. In these instances, the importance of locale in the creation of meaning is evident; exposure of Not Sidney's wealth in Smuteye makes him suspicious, not palatable. As Everett (the character) had earlier asked Not Sidney to recite Sidney Poitier's most famous line from this film: "They call me Mr. Tibbs," Not Sidney finds himself asserting: "They call me Mr. Poitier" (124, 207). What makes both Sidney and Not Sidney palatable in this signifying field is not race or wealth but dignity. The signifier "Sidney Poitier" is often attached to this meaning—the dignified black man—moreso even than to the actor himself. This is clear in the last scene of the novel, when Not Sidney accepts an award as Sidney Poitier; the award is for the "Most Dignified Figure in American Culture" (234). Unfortunately, Not Sidney has no access to "Sidney Poitier" as a structuring signifier in his life, detached from any of the above meanings. Thus, his encounters with "Sidney Poitier" are always attached to the signified, the actor Sidney Poitier.

Not Sidney experiences many moments of identification with the actor Sidney Poitier not through his name but through their physical resemblance; these moments only accentuate Lacan's notion that "the relation to one's own body characterizes . . . the restricted, but really irreducible, field of the imaginary" (11). In the imaginary, Not Sidney's resemblance to the actor Sidney Poitier is self-affirming. When he looks in the mirror, the reflection he sees is the actor Sidney Poitier: "I looked so much like Sidney Poitier that I was momentarily distracted, until I remembered that Sidney Poitier would never have appeared in a scene like this one" (142). As he is receiving fellatio in this moment, he is undoubtedly correct in this assertion; Not Sidney's sexual experiences are nowhere found in Poitier's films. Identification here is with the imaginary other who allows Not Sidney to understand himself as a subject. In another instance, Not Sidney recounts that a group of men "stared at Sidney Poitier's face in the mirror and I stared at it, too. The face in the mirror smiled and I had to smile back" (191). Not Sidney recognizes a separation between himself and the self that smiles at him from the mirror, but is comforted in seeing this other. Only just before his psychotic break does it become clear that this imaginary other may be harmful to Not Sidney's mental well-being. At that time, Not Sidney dreams that he is dead and looking down upon his dead body. When he wakes, he looks in the mirror, where he usually sees the actor Sidney Poitier, and instead sees his face looking "dead enough" (197). In the process of forclusion, to locate the excluded primordial signifier, one can look to the return of that signifier in the real. For Not Sidney Poitier, that return comes with the replaying of this dream, the appearance of his own dead body, yet it is not in a dream, but in the real.

When Not Sidney is brought in by the police to try to identify a dead body, a scene signifying on *In the Heat of the Night*, he believes that the body he sees is his own. This moment considers Julia Kristeva's notion of the abject, suggesting that it is not necessarily (as she contends) disparate from Freudian repudiation, the basis of Lacanian forclusion, but instead that it can be the object not only of "primal repression," but also of primal rejection, or forclusion (Kristeva 12). Kristeva argues that the corpse is an abjection, a "jettisoned object," "radically excluded," that is located "on the edge of non-existence and hallucination, of a reality that, if I acknowledge it, annihilates me" (2). The corpse, as abject, annihilates the subject by bringing what is rejected back into one's reality; this model fits that of Lacan's excluded primordial signifier reappearing in the real. Kristeva argues that the annihilating experience of the abject occurs when the subject "finds the impossible within; when it finds that the impossible constitutes its very *being*," when "it is revealed that all [the subject's] objects are based merely on the inaugural *loss* that laid the foundation of its own being" (5). It seems that this situation could refer no more clearly to the experiences of Not Sidney Poitier and his loss of a primordial signifier. Thus, upon viewing the corpse, he observes:

The man was young, black, with short-cropped hair. His eyes were closed. His lips were slightly parted. He was circumcised. He looked just like me. He looked exactly like me, a fact that was apparently lost on Donald and the Chief. I wanted to say, "That's me." The thought of saying it was strange feeling and scary. My chest was tight, and my ears were ringing. I was lying in the chest, and yet I wasn't. I said, "I don't know him." I was lying, I thought. (211)

While this body does not appear to be Not Sidney Poitier to the other men, to Not Sidney, the dead body is his own. Everett plays with the conception that white people think all black people look alike, thus possibly allowing Donald and the Chief to miss an uncanny resemblance between Not Sidney and the body; however, Not Sidney's panic and confusion suggest that this resemblance is in fact Not Sidney's delusion. The appearance of this corpse, and Not Sidney's ensuing subjective confusion, marks the return of the excluded signifier; it brings to light the effect that the lack of this signifier has had on Not Sidney's subjectivity.[8]

The primordial signifier at the heart of forclusion is that which is to act as the ego's Other in the formation of the subject. A dialectic between ego and Other is necessary for a subject to understand himself as such; the two form an "ellipsis" as the Other provides an answer to the ego's interpellation. That is, the Other "with a big O, that is, the Other in so far as it's not known" is the "you" that one speaks of oneself (Lacan 40). The Other must be acknowledged in order to be integrated into and allow one access to the symbolic order. When the Other is primordially excluded and therefore unable to provide a reply to its interpellation, the subject must form an imaginary relationship with an other in order to maintain a unified conception of the self. For Not Sidney, this relationship was with his mirror image, the actor Sidney Poitier.

The forming of this imaginary relationship is what Lacan (and, originally, Daniel Paul Schreber) refers to as "soul murder" (209). The soul is murdered when the dual relation of the subject is complete only in the imaginary order; "it's insofar as he hasn't acquired or has lost this Other that he encounters the purely imaginary other, the fallen and meager other . . . this other negates him, literally kills him" (209). In this description, the dead body Not Sidney encounters is identified as Not Sidney's other, his imaginary twin that can only cause "pure interdestruction" (305). This destruction is evident as Not Sidney concludes that the twin is in fact himself and that he is in fact dead. This conclusion then paves the way for the return of the excluded in the real, as Not Sidney further surmises that he must be Sidney Poitier: "I thought that if that body in the chest was Not Sidney Poitier, then I was not Not Sidney Poitier and that by all I knew of logic and double negatives, I was therefore Sidney Poitier. I was Sidney Poitier" (212). This does not mean that Not Sidney believes he is *the actor* Sidney Poitier; instead, the signifier has returned free of meaning, allowing Not Sidney to attach it to himself as signified. That is to say, through verbal logic, the excluded signifier "Sidney Poitier" comes to exist in the real, as Not Sidney believes that he is Sidney Poitier, and that Not Sidney Poitier is dead.

Not Sidney's visual delusion is inextricably tied to the verbal in that the exclusionary "Not" of his name is revealed to be the basis of his psychosis. His name's "Not" excludes the signifier "Sidney Poitier"; thus, "Sidney Poitier" is Not Sidney's excluded Other, what could have been the creator of his symbolic order. Thus, when the novel ends with Not Sidney stating that his headstone will say: "*I AM NOT MYSELF TODAY*" he is acknowledging the irreparable divide in his ego, such that "I" and "myself" refer to his ego and Other, which can never be reconciled. At this point, Not Sidney acknowledges that the basis of his missing Other is in his name, stating: "I came back to this place to find something, to connect with something lost, to reunite if not with my whole self, then with a piece of it. What I've discovered is that this thing is not here. In fact, it is nowhere. I have learned that my name is not my name" (234). In its failure to name him such that he can respond to interpellation with "I am," Not Sidney's name is not his name. This linguistic conclusion is supported by the hypothesis Not Sidney unknowingly made earlier, which aligned Sidney Poitier with the order of the father in the space of the unknown Other. "Sidney Poitier" as signifier could have structured Not Sidney's symbolic order, but was excluded such that Not Sidney could not attribute symbolic meaning to himself or the world around him.

Thus, although Not Sidney appears to be "normal" throughout the novel, his final delusion reveals that he had been compensating for the exclusion of a primordial signifier. This does not mean that he is completely psychotic; rather, it suggests only that he is partially delusional due to a rupture in his symbolic order. This rupture is based in language, but appears in the material dimensions of his life as well. The essential signifier

in Not Sidney Poitier's life is locatable as part of his name, "Sidney Poitier," which is also the Name-of-the-Father, philosophically and potentially
literally. This signifier trumps all others—those of race, class, age, and so
on—in determining the course of his life, because it is this signifier that
disallows him from speaking his being, responding to his interpellation
with "I," and thus creating a symbolic order. Percival Everett (the author)
has managed to assert the importance of race as a signifying category at
the same time as he rejects it as the essential signifier. He presents blackness among differing webs of signifying fields that change its meaning.
Above all, he allows readers to think of the experience of being a young,
rich, attractive, black man both within and outside of the boundaries of
those signifying categories. That is to say, one can read the dilemma of Not
Sidney Poitier's life not as stemming from any of those identity categories,
but rather from a primordial exclusion based in language.

Through its representation in Everett's novel, forclusion is helpful in
theorizing race as one of many important signifiers, such that it becomes
impossible to essentialize "the black experience," which changes with every conceivable signifying field. At the same time, the novel helps to theo-
rize further forclusion; by adding the visuality of resemblance to Lacan's
theory, Everett forces a consideration of the place of the body—including the racialized body—in the creation of reality, especially as the body
is understood through the interworkings of the linguistic and the visual,
and as the meanings attached to signifiers are so often dependent on the
visual. Further, by making visible Lacan's linguistic argument, through the
use of Not Sidney's name, and paralleling that argument with a material
counterpart, his actual missing father, Everett allows for some confusion
around the relationship of the two, and thus the relative influence of each
on subject formation. This is at once a productive confusion, as it allows a
consideration of the politics of naming and the influence of the material
on language and vice versa, as well as a potentially dangerous confusion, as
it begins to meld the symbolic and real fathers, leaving single or "hysterical" mothers to blame for psychosis.[9] The novel provides an exploration
of the merits of forclusion as a theory of subjectivity and uses the divide
between signifier and signified, central to forclusion, to demonstrate that
the web of signification that is reality must be understood as such in order
to grasp the complexities of black being—and black writing—in America.

Notes

1. The concept, developed in Lacan's seminar "The Psychoses," is based on Sigmund Freud's *verwerfung;* Lacan uses this term throughout the seminar, but ultimately departs from it, stating: "I propose to you definitively to adopt this translation which I believe is the best—foreclosure" (321). According to Dany Nobus, Lacan chose this translation because it "epitomized the exclusion of a linguistic element (a signifier) rather than an 'internal perception'" (16). Utilizing the untranslated "forclusion" to refer specifically to Lacan's ideas—for, as his seminar demonstrates, meaning is produced through the signifier—this essay recognizes the greasy shifting of signifier and signified and aims to retain as closely as possible Lacan's meaning.

2. See Freud's article "Negation" in James Strachey, ed., *The Standard Edition of the Complete Psychological Works of Sigmund Freud*, 19 (1925): 235–39.

3. Not Sidney concludes that his mother must have been "hysterically pregnant" with him for about fourteen months before becoming "actually" pregnant (5). For more on the fantasy of pregnancy in adult women, see Julia Kristeva's *The Sense and Non-Sense of Revolt* (New York: Columbia University Press, 2000).

4. The two exceptions to this rule occur through accent and accident: in the first instance, a man speaking with a British accent says: "Are you not Sidney Poitier?" to which Not Sidney can reply: "I am" (231). The second case centers on a woman's confusion upon reading Not Sidney's name; she asks: "You're not Sidney Poitier?" Again, Not Sidney can answer, "I am" (232). In both instances, Not Sidney must choose to ignore what he knows is a misunderstanding of his name in order to speak his being. In this situation, speaking his being rings somewhat false due to the confusion.

5. Along with the naming of her son, Not Sidney's mother's hysteria could be said to have caused the primordial exclusion of his father in that she attempted to take the father's place in the symbolic order. The suggestion that single motherhood is a precursor for the psychoses of children is clearly problematic; however, Everett lets Lacan's line of reasoning remain unchanged in order to explore forclusion in its original form. For more of Lacan's ideas on the absence of the father as the cause of psychosis, see "The Family Complexes," trans. Carolyn Asp, in *Critical Texts* 5, no. 3 (1988): 12–29.

6. The one story within the black literary tradition that relates most clearly to Not Sidney's dilemma is Ralph Waldo Ellison's "Hidden Name and Complex Fate," in which Ellison identifies his own burdensome name as formative in his development as a writer. To overcome the difficulties presented by his name's association with Ralph Waldo Emerson, he shortened his middle name to "W." He states: "I did not destroy that troublesome middle name of mine, I only suppressed it" (166). This

suppression is necessary for Ellison to constitute his subjectivity, and his identity as a writer. Conversely, in choosing not to suppress any part of his name, Not Sidney is unable to overcome the lack that it inaugurates.

7. Lacan developed a theory of lack over the course of many years; he saw the lack of an object as the cause of desire. While this object could be the imaginary phallus, the real breast, or the symbolic phallus, Lacan was most interested in the lack of the imaginary phallus, which led to symbolic castration. For the purposes of this essay, Lacanian lack refers to the lack of a signifier in the Other, a "pure" signifier that provides access to the symbolic order, as explained fully in his seminar "La relation d'objet" of 1956–57 and utilized in "The Psychoses."

8. Whereas Lacan's seminar focuses on the return of the Other as a speaking Other, a voice that only the subject hears, the novel suggests that not only verbal delusion, but also visual delusion is possible through forclusion. This projection of one's delusion into the body of another is similar to Lacan's account of the woman who hears a man say: "Sow!" (Lacan 52). This moment could also be read to signify on W. E. B. Du Bois's signifier—if not signified—double consciousness. Not Sidney sees himself not as fragments, but as impossibly doubled.

9. The blaming of black single mothers for their children's problems, absent a consideration of historical, cultural, and societal factors beyond the control of these women, has become a kind of American tradition. For the most famous example, see Daniel Patrick Moynihan's *The Negro Family: The Case for National Action* (1965).

Chapter 3

Frenzy
Framing Text to Set Discourse in a Cultural Continuum

RONALD DORRIS

[S]omeone in each era must make clear the facts with utter disregard to his own wish and desire and belief. What we have got to know, as far as possible, are the things that actually happened in the world . . . the historian has no right posing as a scientist to conceal or distort facts; and until we distinguish between the two functions of the chronicler of human action, we are going to render it easy for a muddled world out of sheer ignorance to make the same mistake ten time over.

—W. E. B. DU BOIS, "The Propaganda of History," *Black Reconstruction* (1935)

Percival Everett's *Frenzy* (1997), modeled on the storyline of *The Bacchae* by Euripides, is a postmodern revision of the story of the god of wine, madness, fertility, and ecstasy, Dionysos.[1] The narrator of Everett's novel informs us that in the midst of the "frenzied Bakkhanal,"[2] the story of Dionysos is told through Vlepo, "an unfrenzied observer" (3) without form that manifests only at the command of Dionysos. Vlepo says of himself, "I was there to tell the participants what it was they enjoyed or did. My usual place was at the side of the god Bromius as his aide, his chronicler, his mortal bookmark. I am Vlepo" (3).

Vlepo without form serves as chronicler of bacchic unfolding. As a governing definition for this analysis, that which is bacchic is connoted as the attempt on the part of a people in an uprooted environment to balance emotion and intellect, which encompasses growth pattern bound in the rhythms of organic life and all its integral variations. From this base, this analysis engages Percival Everett's *Frenzy* not as fiction centered on

protagonist(s) and antagonist(s), but as the framing of *text* to a set discourse in a cultural continuum. This continuum references the cross-cultural connections between Afro-Asiatic and Greek cultures. *In Santeria from
Africa to the New World: The Dead Sell Memories* (1993), George Brandon
offers a perspective centered on the emergence of such discourse:

> In a cultural continuum the differences in thought and behavior derive
> from a shared pool of ideology, history, myth and experience. But people
> relate to this shared pool differently because of their place in society and
> because of their place on the continuum. Thus these differences can be
> used as a way for people to represent themselves to others and to them-
> selves. Into this shared pool fall racial and ethnic concepts, stereotypes,
> and images, the relationships between symbols and economic and politi-
> cal power on the one hand, and tradition and self-identity on the other.
> The reality of the intersystem then is the bridges of transformations nec-
> essary to get from one end of the intersystem to the other. (Brandon 161)

Euripides's *The Bacchae*, which frames Everett's novel, complements Brandon's perspective relative to a cultural continuum. Dionysos as a principle character in *Frenzy* is the character positioned as understudy, rather
than the sole chronicler of his tale. Correspondingly, the emphasis that
is placed on how each chronicler in *Frenzy* addresses that importance of
command of the WORD to tell the tale is what gives life to and shapes
Frenzy's bacchic unfolding. It is an unfolding that mirrors a postmodern
narrative aesthetic underpinned by fragmentation and multivalent truths
about the lives and histories of all of the characters. In the novel, Dionysos
is immersed in conflict with other characters; and as understudy in the
text, he is also immersed in conflict with himself. His discursive engagement with himself and others centers not only on his ulterior motive to
understand what constitutes love but also to learn how love feels or how
one feels love. The characters in the novel—what I call sermon-voices—Dionysos, Pentheus, Kadmos, and Semele, Agave, and the maddened women
aid in an examination of Dionysos as understudy central to Everett's textual framing in *Frenzy*.

Everett's employment of *The Bacchae* as a frame for his novel is not un-
precedented in an African American literary and historical continuum,

although his approach is certainly unique. A number of African American writers specifically mention *The Bacchae*; hence, they identify the frame up front; among others, *The Bacchae* as literary frame is implied. For example, in Claude McKay's *Home to Harlem* (1928), Nella Larsen's *Quicksand* (1928), Jessie Redmon Fauset's *The Chinaberry Tree* (1931), and Paule Marshall's *Brown Girl, Brownstones* (1959), *The Bacchae* specifically is mentioned and/or bacchic unfolding is identified. In Jean Toomer's *Cane* (1923), *The Bacchae* as textual frame is implied.[3] Much like these works that have received little or no analysis of *The Bacchae* as framing discourse, *Frenzy* has been likewise understudied.

In "Signing to the Blind," Everett shares his feelings about his position as an African American writer. He notes: "Many of us make good livings writing. The problem that economic censorship presents is a hushing of ideas and indeed the censorship itself is merely a symptom of the insidious political disease which infects our culture" (Everett 9). Everett relates that in 1983 Embassy Pictures optioned the film rights to his first novel, *Suder* (1983), "written about an African-American's internal search for emancipation" (9). The movie was never done. Despite all changes to the potential production, based on hearsay Everett surmises that the script was not "white" enough. He offers commentary:

> Since that time I have reacted, in my cranky way, by writing two novels which purposely do not overtly specify the race of the main characters. *Walk Me to the Distance* is about alienation, the division of and search for family and a search for spiritual and physical location and yet I read in some magazine article that I was avoiding the hard stuff of "black life." I know that the majority of our readership is simple-minded, but to miss these themes as central to the African American experience is too much. And to assume the race of the character betrays not only an unsophisticated eye which cannot read symbolically, but the insidious colonialist reader's eye which infects America. And it is here that the problem lies. (10)

Thus, in his work, Everett redirects his frustrations through his creative energy in order to shift reaction to generate an answer to the general "blindness" of critics and readers to the plentitude of African American

experiential and literary interests. His response, as in all of his work, surfaces in *Frenzy*, a novel steeped in both African American and Western literary traditions. None of the characters in the novel is race-specific; they
could very well be of Afro-Asiatic descent. At any rate, design and discourse
of the novel certainly complements the African American oral tradition.
His approach and technique can be better understood relative to theory
posited by Cheryl Wharry in "Amen and Hallelujah Preaching: Discourse
Functions in African American Sermons." Wharry points out, "The few
studies that have taken discourse approaches to sermon analysis typically
have analyzed seminary-trained white preachers" (Wharry 203). She provides further clarification central to oral and written text:

> Traditional African American sermons are typically NOT first written
> and do not command their value in the context of WRITTEN LITERA-
> TURE. They do not conform to the criterion of being initially "reduced"
> (a word that might be selected by those who find orality more meaning-
> ful than literacy in their communities) to the written word. Because of
> the multiple cultural functions of the spoken word, African Americans
> have tended to value oral performance much more highly than do cul-
> tures that are closer to the literate end of the literary-orality continuum.
> (204)

Everett contextualizes his personal sermon and that of characters in
Frenzy closer to the literary-orality continuum by positioning the sermons
as respective oral performances that draw from versions of *The Bacchae*
handed down from generation to generation as written texts. Those written texts have surfaced with focus on Thebes, Egypt (Heredotus), Thebes,
Greece (Euripides), Nigeria (Soyinka), and the United States (McKay, Lars-
en, Marshall, and Toomer, among others). Hence Everett's setting of text
as discourse in a continuum in *Frenzy* endows the work, among other approaches, as a cross-cultural feast equal to any bacchic unfolding on any
transnational stage.

In *The Bacchae* Dionysos takes center stage as a transplant who seeks
to establish his divinity in Thebes, working his way westward into Greece
as he travels out of Asia and across Egypt with a band of followers. Keeping with Wharry's postulate, in *Frenzy* we see "textual boundary marker,

spiritual maintenance filler, rhythmic marker, and the infrequent call-response marker" (203). Aligning *Frenzy* for critical analysis with Wharry's theory, Everett's achievement is identifiable given "results that support the importance of the role that culture (here, African/African American oral traditions) plays in sermon performance. (African American English, sermons, religious discourse, discourse analysis, discourse markers, genre)" (203). Thus Everett's handling of bacchic unfolding as the frame for *Frenzy* demonstrates his mastery of manipulating the language. Everett manipulates language to revise discourses on history, collective memory, space, time, and place that plague the characters in *Frenzy*.

From the outset, we are aware of the manner in which Everett is framing text in *Frenzy* when Vlepo exclaims:

In time, all time, I hate my Bakkhos, love my Bakkhos. I am lost in the counting of his moments, and report in slow detail to him that which happens in a flash. I see a love before me, not mine, though, for I have found no life in this body. Body? Dare I call it such? Lashed to the god by his words, his lips forming his pain and play like a song, and I spit it back at him, loving my Bakkhos, my god. (3–4)

Should he be able to identify what constitutes love, Dionysos hopes to vindicate the honor of his mother, a mortal woman, who was killed by a flash of lightning at his birth when she declared that he had been fathered by the god Zeus. As discourse is advanced in *Frenzy*, in the exchange between members of the House of Kadmos, we observe that Dionysos cannot solve the riddle of what constitutes love because he does not know the story that governs the house. Thus, Dionysos's understanding of his own history, his birth, is fragmented and up for conjecture. Dionysos enters the House of Kadmos, the mortal side of family, as a transplant from the outside, and relies on his supernatural familiar and bookmark, Vlepo, to be his guide and interpreter, which, in turn, deprive him of amassing and making sense of his own experience.

Herodotus acknowledges in *Euterpe*, the second book of his four-volume *History*, the apparent origin of bacchic worship in Thebes, Egypt, and that through cross-cultural exchanges, the ceremony was later transferred to Thebes, Greece.[4] In his African version of *The Bacchae of Euripides: A*

Communion Rite (1973), Wole Soyinka, 1986 recipient of the Nobel Prize for Literature, discusses the bacchic principle as a dramatic statement that captures a particular moment in a people's history, a moment so infinite, says Soyinka, that it becomes imbued in the Eternal Present.[5] Isidore Okpewho offers commentary on Soyinka's work in "Soyinka, Euripides, and the Anxiety of Empire." Okpewho declares that he has chosen to see Soyinka's effort as a translation of culture, not of text. He bases his declaration on the energy he accepts Soyinka put into the ethnos and ethos relative to manipulating the language of the play.[6]

Framed in the context of *The Bacchae*, Everett, too, casts developments in *Frenzy* in the Eternal Present. The Eternal Present encompasses embrace of the belief that there is neither past nor future; all that one ever will have is the moment that one has. For if one were to say "I was," one is saying, "I am not now"; and if one were to say, "I will be," one is saying, "I have yet to become." In *Frenzy*, Dionysos confirms his embrace of the Eternal Present to Vlepo. He tells him:

> I must relive for example, my birth, my mother's death, my mother's seduction, and every pain and lost feeling of my first breath. To compound it all, my recollection and time inhabit the same fissure of space, so all time before and after me exists for me, at all times. Is this difficult for your mind, Vlepo? (10)

In *Frenzy* Everett remains true to the master text of *The Bacchae* but manipulates the story enough for his own purposes—that of demonstrating cultural continuity across time and space. The play opens with focus on a chorus that follows Dionysos from Asia Minor as he enters Thebes, Greece, the land of his mortal mother. His aim is to address displacement and to vindicate the honor of his mother, Semele, by convincing citizens of Thebes that she conceived him with Zeus as his father. At odds with Dionysos is his first cousin, Pentheus, king of Thebes, who believes that state authority and order are being undermined and threatened by his cousin's push for what seems to be evolving into a new religion. Dionysos clearly and emphatically asserts his divinity and proudly insists that he will be recognized in Thebes, and then move on. Only if opposition to him is violent and unyielding, says Dionysos, only if the established order resorts to force against his initiated bacchants who follow him from Asia into Thebes will he array himself against this order.

The established order, given their misidentification of those who follow Dionysus, does resort to force against the initiated bacchants. Those immersed in the rites of Bacchus, such as the women who follow Dionysos from Asia into Thebes, Greece, are *bacchants*. The Theban women, uninitiated in the rites, are driven mad from their homes and flock to the hills of Cithaeron. In their madness, they are now called *maenads*. Both groups consume wine, a potent symbol of bacchic worship. Wine releases the purely external inhibitions on conduct. Wine releases the elemental urges of the human heart, the deep passions of men and women, Eros and Desire in the widest sense. These include the sexual, but spread far beyond the sexual. The chief revelation of the bacchic rite is that once independent passions collectively are recognized each claims center stage as the source of all loveliness and joy. But if one fights against instead of with the passions, declare the bacchants, they will be conquered in the end, torn limb from limb by the uninitiated, the latter becoming ugly and fiendish in the process. Much of what unfolds in the novel is told through the mind's eye of Dionysos's servant, Vlepo.

Frenzy chronicles Vlepo in space, and Vlepo is aware of his limitations. He cannot transport time and place via collective memory because he is not his own creation, nor is he created in the likeness and image of another force, but trapped between a mortal and a divine fabricated image of himself. As an understudy in search of what constitutes love, Dionysos continually is shortchanged in his quest because he is divorced from himself as his own mortal bookmark. Says Vlepo:

> For as long as I have known that there is time and a life to know, I have been with the god. I am not his creation, but I cannot claim a life away from him. My experience is, of a kind, my own, but it is shaped by what is chosen for me to see. I watch the others, the mortals, whom I assume are like me except in the way I am bound to my Bakkhos, bound by space and idea. (3)

Bound by space and idea and not time and place, Dionysos is not connected to, and does not interact with the Thebean community, nor does he have a direct hand in establishing his new theology within the community. Certain philosophers say *experience* serves as the basis for creation. If experience does not serve as the basis for creation, the least and the most that we fabricate about life would seem to stem from how we are conditioned to "create" from social construction as a base. Vlepo cannot bring to Dionysos the answers that the latter seeks about what constitutes love because as a form without body, Vlepo cannot experience. And were he able to do so, he would be trying to share what he experiences with a Dionysos who, likewise, has no collective memory to shape experience. In order to know what love is, Dionysos needs to draw from collective memory borne from the dead and the living.

Dionysos is a transplant who marches into Thebes under the banner of *hearsay* about all that happened to his mother; Dionysos has not experienced what happened to his mother. Dionysos's nonexperiential status projects him not as independent subject, but as the object of someone else's ridicule. Likewise, Vlepo is the object of Dionysos's ridicule because the latter can make him assume any form to carry out any dehumanizing act in order to explain whether or not he is moving toward feeling and understanding of what constitutes love.

Relative to Thebes, Dionysos holds his own fabricated sense of history in his mind. He has no experience of the history of Thebes and cannot engage this history because he has not lived this history. He was ripped from his dead mother's womb, nurtured in the thigh of Zeus, and has grown up in isolation/exile away from the history of Thebes. Says Vlepo, "On a slab of reality in the mind of Dionysos, where he held the history of his time . . . on that plane did the god allow me access to him as companion" (8). Dionysus tells of his origin through the mixing of god and human, Zeus and Semele. But how far can we trust his version of the story? Vlepo points out, "He told how that was the story, anyway, though he had heard stories that contradicted that one" (9). Here Everett makes us aware that there are many conflicting stories about Dionysos. And those conflicting stories will continue to surface from others because Dionysos himself exerts no command of personal memory essential to offering reinforcement as a necessary component of collective memory.

Past, present, and future, Vlepo is permitted to see Dionysos unravel action that he thinks surrounds the version of the imagined history about his mother, Semele, in order to justify the bacchic means he uses to try to touch base with love to know what his mother experienced and suffered. Much ground is covered before Vlepo reaches an understanding. "My Bakkhos would have made a terrible weaver," Vlepo admits. "What I had thought was a tapestry of his time and space was a pile of threads, a mound of twisted temporality subject to no rule or logic. If there were some strategy, I could not comprehend it. I was left not to fill in the gaps and holes but to make them, to create spaces where I could see and attempt to understand or to pursue some distinct narrative thread" (73).

Dionysos is his own misguided model in *Frenzy*. What he is weaving, or thinks he is weaving, amounts to nothing more than "a mound of twisted temporality subject to no rule or logic" (73). Confused about what has happened in the past, and with no sense of history in the present, Dionysos does not project as a model that can proffer a vision for the future. "Temporality" would be enough to overshadow him, but "twisted temporality" sounds his own death knell, as well as the death he will array against others if they reject a religion he wants to impose upon them unrooted in any sense of foundation, let alone their sense of history. Dionysos had made up his mind before he entered Thebes that Pentheus dare not challenge him. In "Dionysus in the *Bacchae*," George Maximilian Antony Gube writes, "But instead of opposing Pentheus in war, he adopts a more cruel and also a more tragic plan. It is over the mind of Pentheus himself that he will establish his sway; it is in the king's own soul that the power of the god will make itself felt" (Grube 49).

Everett is masterful in his choice of language to show the limits of what Dionysos proposes for his salvation and the salvation of others. *Frenzy* puts forth that Dionysos does not come bearing a religion free of charge. One pays a heavy price for joining his "order." First of all, he brings with him to Thebes those who have been initiated in his rites, yet they do not offer such instruction for the citizens of Thebes. Those who follow him into Thebes do so blindly. If indeed humankind is created in the likeness and image of God embraced as a higher force, it is reasoned that God is inside of each of us. *Frenzy* shows us a Dionysos of which no one is created in his likeness and image because Dionysus does not live inside anyone, even though he physically pushes his frenzy inside many, men and women, in a mad desire to experience love. The only thing Dionysos offers to those who blindly follow him is wine, his bacchic symbol; and without proper instruction and guidance, the uninitiated become intoxicated and destroy rather than create. Thus we learn that even his gift of wine is not free, nor does it lead one to freedom. The people pay for this wine with their blood and the blood of others, never having known the power of love.

We now turn to Pentheus, whose name is emblematic of the five senses. How could Pentheus ever experience love and express love for his own spiritual uplift, his family, his state, or his station as king given that he dismisses the past? Without a past, and certainly of his own choosing, he is no better than Dionysos as a model when it comes to offering a constructive sermonic discourse. For Pentheus, whatever is done is done. From his perspective, let the dead lie low and stay buried. What is above earth must be embraced at the moment that it is embraced. For him there is nothing else. Unlike the other players in *Frenzy*, all engaged in carnal love, Pentheus never consummates the act. Rather than being loved, his people fear him: "A rumbling of whispers among the few men on the street announced the arrival of Pentheus, son of Echion and Kadmos' daughter Agave, and so, in fact, cousin of Bromius" (6).

The first exclamation of Pentheus as king is that he will send warriors to the forest, have Dionysos captured, and cut off all his hair for the women to see how small he is and hence clear their vision. Commentary on this development is presented in Andrea J. Nouryeh's "Soyinka's Euripides: Postcolonial Resistance or Avant-Garde Adaptation":

> The impulsiveness and cruel, unmeasured power that the young King Pentheus exercises in concern with his ability to recognize the sensuousness and irrationality of Dionysos within himself are the qualities that unleash the same uncontrolled forces of will in the god . . . . Nor does this underscore Pentheus's outrage at the sexuality that Dionysos unleashes but it places the young king in the position of being the only one who refuses to believe in the existence, let alone the deity of his cousin and submit to his rites. Thus he becomes the only obstacle for Dionysos worship and its promise of freedom, equality, and plenty for the community. (166–68)

The blind prophet Tiresias, dressed in full bacchic regalia as a visitor standing before Kadmos, takes on the role of teacher to see if he can help swing the tide: "We depend in this world on the good provided us by Demeter. Be warned, Pentheus, that Dionysos is at least equal to Mother Earth in power. It is he, from Zeus and Semele, who brings us the gift of wine, that medicine which empowers us to forget the length of these tedious days, to find the deep and peaceful sleep, to dismiss our pains. There is no other cure for our condition. You would keep us from the roots of our creation, from the breathing parent of our material constitution?" (7).

Both Tiresias and Kadmos attempt to show Pentheus that preoccupation with his urge to exercise imperial rule, and disavowal of all things foreign with which the kingdom comes into contact, threatens the kingdom from within. The elders accept that the kingdom is rooted in time and place, not in the space bound by Pentheus's preoccupation with establishing, administering, and maintaining imperial power and the status quo. Admonishment of Pentheus by his elders that he should learn to sit in communion with his fellows, both the dead and the living, calls to mind Wole Soyinka's adaptation of *The Bacchae*. Okpewho proffers that a historicist response crafted by Soyinka in his adaptation accounts for discomfort arising from challenges between ancestral traditions and imperial culture (Okpewho 33).

For Pentheus the state comes before all else. As heir to the throne and a proponent of imperial culture, he wants to structure a life for Thebes while disavowing that Thebes already envelops life. If he is to be his own architect as well as the architect of Thebes, he must first understand that "It is useful to look at the cultural continuum as having two levels of structure, external and internal [and that] . . . the internal variation within the continuum contributes some of its most important characteristics and gives rise to a number of situations that seem confusing, contradictory, and anomalous but which are very common" (Brandon 162).

In our search for common ground that gives rise to angles of consistency in *Frenzy*, it is now clear that Everett's staging of *The Bacchae* as frame for *Frenzy* impacts our gaze to examine the work of Euripides "from an abstract appreciation of this notion of temporal soup to an applied comprehension" (10). This sense of understanding further becomes clear given the echo of Vlepo that the tapestry of Dionysos shows him as a "terrible weaver" (73), because his tapestry "is a mound of twisted temporality subject to no rule or logic" (73).

Temporality, from the Latin *temporalitas*, pertains to church possessions. Dionysos, feeling that the honor of his mother continues to be desecrated and that habitually he is scorned, seeks his due by virtue of wanting others to acknowledge his divinity by embracing what he wants to establish as a new religion in Thebes.

Everett's stable footing in *Frenzy* does not rest on delivery alone, but in the context of the bearer of the delivery. *Frenzy* illuminates that the men in Thebes do not transport life, as is the case with no man on the planet Earth. Women are the bearers of life, transporting that form through nine months of darkness until they lead life toward the light. Aching to be free from adulterated burdens of history and tradition, in *Frenzy* the women seem disinterested in taking control as architects of their own destiny. On the surface it seems that wine as bacchic symbol induces a frenzy that maddens the women in Thebes and drives them from their respective home. But wine is not the culprit. Loosened by wine and exhausted from a feast of flesh and worship, the blind prophet Tiresias sits among the women and redirects discourse from focus on the external cultural continuum to the internal cultural continuum: "We Greeks speak so pompously of reason," he says, "yet things to which we direct said thinking are all matters of guessing. We are not thinkers, we are gamblers . . . . Democracy is such a sightless word, a condition rather than a practice, easily spoken of by its participants and drooled over by its estranged. Take the way you women have been treated. . . ." (43).

The perspective on the mistreatment of women advanced by Tiresias constitutes a dramatic shift in *Frenzy*. Now we are aware that all the drunken revelry, debauchery, and physical dismemberment in *Frenzy* had been escalating so that the spotlight is directed on theoretical as opposed to applied democracy. Everett has been prepping us to accompany Vlepo, who is transformed into a louse, and who attaches himself to Agave's scalp so that he can read her thoughts and share in her sermon/concern: *O Bakkhos, my Bakkhos! The gift of the vine will allow me and my sisters to haze away the vision of our treatment, to swim in your sweet delirium. How we thrive away from those rodents called men! . . . . They talk petty philosophy with their whores into the night, kissing boys and petting themselves into corners, all with no master to pay* (44). Vlepo does not take credit for this dramatic shift, relegating the honor to his host when he exclaims, "Dionysos put me upon the head of Agave. The window into her thinking was buried beneath her gray hairs, but I found stable footing and observed" (43).

We now can avoid any further circuitous route of traveling through *Frenzy* because now we are aware that apart from wanting to establish his divinity Dionysos's search to embrace and to understand love is rooted in gender conflict that impacts the citizens of Thebes. The undisputed fact that Dionysos does not celebrate—others celebrate—shows him longing for a life he will never acquire. In addition to establishing his divinity, Dionysos also is in Thebes hoping to learn from his mother's alleged rejection by Zeus what constitutes lost love. By experiencing love, perhaps he hopes to know what his mother felt for Zeus.

There is no confirmation that Dionysos is a member of the divine pantheon. This simply is a claim he is attempting to establish. His mother was mortal. As the daughter of a king, she was expected to name the father of her unborn child. She did not name a mortal man; she named the god Zeus. If she had blasphemed the god, she was struck by a lightning bolt. If she had told the truth, she was taken into heaven by a streak of lightning. As a mortal, she is buried on earth, her tomb surrounded by an eternal flame. Thus, like her son, her "history" is enmeshed in ambiguity.

Any focus on Semele in *Frenzy* keeps her story wedded as an idea in space. Vlepo informs us of this stance:

> The move from an abstract appreciation of this notion of temporal soup to an applied comprehension of its being as such was bound to be jarring. The god permitted me, or perhaps subjected me, to a viewing of one of the constant threads of his existence. I found myself situated in the fetus Dionysos, located inside the womb of his mother Semele. (10)

At this station, Vlepo is transfixed by Hera, jealous wife of Zeus. He recalls, "[S]he looked at me, there with the spirit of Dionysos, locating us in the air and cementing us in space . . . . Reference being tethered to the event of discourse, I found myself wrenched away from one thread to another" (12).

The closest Dionysos can get to understanding what a woman feels, how she feels on the inside within her darkness, is to send his mortal bookmark into her head. In his last desperate attempt to see women see the *light*, hence to get women to see each other as well as men and women each to see the other, Dionysos himself goes to the underworld to commune with his mother Semele. When Dionysus calls out the name of Semele, seven "ghosts" stand. He says to Vlepo, "Bring them all, and we will sort her out later . . . . And there, as we grew near the world of the living, second in line was Semele, her beauty finding patter, her eyes locating focus" (147).

Unable to get the truth about his mother, Dionysos eventually accepts help from his mortal bookmark and cries out twice to Vlepo, "My mother is beneath the world" (132). Unlike Euripides's version, in *Frenzy* Dionysos travels to the underworld in search of his mother, "but there is no activity. Instead, they all stood like statues posed badly but locked in space with an esoteric kind of symmetry" (132). Dionysos's version of the story is posed badly and locked in space. Given that he is not rooted in time and place, Dionysos cannot breathe life into any version of the story that he comes up with about his mother, neither above nor below ground.

In the underworld, Dionysos presents a stick of myrtle wood to Persephone so that she may release his mother to him. She does so without a fuss, her myrtle wood of more importance to her. But among the mass without form, Dionysos does not recognize his mother. When he calls her name, only when the seven figures who stand and are led toward the light does his mother, second in line, begin to take shape. But to hide her from the jealous Hera, wife of Zeus, Dionysos rechristens his mother Thyone. Semele accepts her new name from her son, exclaiming, "Thyone? I am Thyone? I will be who I must to breathe this air. Thyone?" (149). Dionysos, now with Semele as compliant, secures establishing a false sense of history relative to Thebes.

Prior to going to the underworld to retrieve his mother, to retrieve that which transported him into the light, Dionysos has been failing to establish the story of Semele. And the form that he beckons to follow him from the underworld he cannot sort out. Among the seven forms that answer to his summons, we have no guarantee even when the second in line stands up and claims she is Semele that she is authentic. Not even Dionysus is certain. Simply, he rationalizes that to steer the memory of his mother away from further misdirected discourse, he will ascribe to this latest configuration a false identity. Here *Frenzy* suggests, once again, that because Dionysos is rooted in space—whether the world of the living or the world of the dead—and not in time and place, he is unable to formulate any understanding about what constitutes love. *Frenzy*, cast in the frame of *The Bacchae*, augments this deficit by shifting the spotlight to Agave instead of Semele because the former, to remain immersed in the light, does not allow the men to divorce her from her sense of not her own but their shortcomings.

Throughout *Frenzy* role reversal permeates as pronounced signifier, and underscores discourse on gender conflict. Dionysos may look as demure as any woman, given his "feminine brow" (4), but he is not a woman. Neither in *The Bacchae* nor in *Frenzy* is he presented as a woman. Both works show that his antics can induce others to transform, but he cannot. In *The Bacchae*, the men haze the women, sending them though continual tortuous fire not to assert but to undermine their worth. In *Frenzy* the role is reversed, and the women haze the men. The struggle of the women to amass empowerment is echoed by Agave. We learn of her concern once Dionysos mounts Vlepo atop her head for observation. She thinks, *This gift of the vine will allow me and my poor sisters to haze away the vision of our treatment* (44). The men deny the women the power to be architects to fashion a sense of history borne of collective memory. Agave is aware that *"This dancing scares them, these strings of movement mock their stillness, and they, say, 'come back here, you women; come back, you property'"* (44). Agave's dance scares the men because "Habit memory is concerned not with facts but with actions, not with the cognitive knowledge of rules or codes but with the ability to exercise mental and physical skills" (Brandon 130–31).

The heat of misunderstanding stifles the air in Thebes, and will permeate continuously until there is some consensus between the men and women about what constitutes their shared sense of history. In Thebes the women are not allowed to transmit their light, so they transmit their bodies. Their calling up and command of habit-memory accounts for conflict in Thebes, and this bone of contention overrides development of a sense of collective memory for all citizens.

Semele had come up with a plan to override negation of her light. As the "beauty of nature" favored by Zeus, she asked him to grant her one wish. Vlepo takes us into the head of Semele to witness her "gazing deep into a well of light" (14), as she questions her demand and her choice: *Does my love hide himself because I am not worthy of full experience of him? I cannot move surreptitiously about him and expect view, nor should I want view by such furtive means. I want my love to show me himself, to let me fail, if I must, to measure up to his beauty and magnificence* (14-15).

Zeus granted Semele her one wish without knowing what would erupt as consequence of the request. When she asked to see his light, he could not back out on his promise, but Semele was killed by that light, which entrenches her tomb as an eternal flame. The fight between Zeus and Semele as emblematic of light and darkness is all-encompassing and consuming. To *haze* means to irritate, vex, and insult. It is conceivable that Semele irritated, vexed, and insulted Zeus by asking him to reveal his light. Had he shown his light and she had gained firsthand knowledge about its source, perhaps he would have lost his power. Could it be that Zeus reversed the threat by irritating, vexing, and insulting Semele, and then struck her with a lightning bolt? Likewise, it may be that all who continue to support her claim that her request to see the light was not unreasonable, and therefore continue to pay homage to her plight as well, are maddened from their homes.

To *haze* also means to frighten, scold, or beat, as well as to loiter or ramble aimlessly. As *Frenzy* opens in the frame of *The Bacchae*, Tiresias rambles aimlessly to the palace to engage his good friend Kadmos in discourse on the women. Kadmos is dressed in a manner like the followers of Dionysos: "a dappled fawnskin, a thyrsus, and a wig of flowing hair" (4). Kadmos admonishes Tiresias for looking silly, exclaiming, "Let it not be said that there is no humor left in Thebes" (4). Humor aside, Tiresias counsels that a greater danger threatens the kingdom. He warns, "Your women are gone to join those who follow and worship the god Bromius. They have gone to beat the loose-skinned drum of life and power, leaving your city, shall we say, male" (4-5). Herein smolders the conflict.

As Agave deems them, a city full of "rodents called men" (44), who cannot transport life from darkness to light, and who preempt those who can, the men leave themselves without a foundation to set discourse on history upheld by collective memory. Hence the hazing continues. The city as ship is not safely anchored. Relative to nautical terminology, *haze* means to harass by exacting unnecessary, disagreeable, or difficult work. According to Agave, the men of Thebes require much of the women, and none is the wiser. Nor do they benefit from the effort. Minus mutual and genuine exchange, much is torn limb from limb.

Chaos escalates and frustration reigns. Dionysos cannot establish his divinity, vindicate the honor of his mother, nor understand anything about love because he is outside the history of Thebes. The story of Semele cannot provide stable footing because we get it from Dionysos, who tells so many versions that we do not know which to believe. Agave retorts that to secure genuine exchange, experience must be channeled through the collective memory of women, the transporters of life whose light continually is snuffed out by the men. In his effort to secure genuine exchange, Tiresias attempts, as seer, to bridge with his wisdom both the world of the men and the women, but each side scoffs at him. We are jarred by another twist in the plot when Agave, in whom Vlepo declares that he finds "stable footing" for observation, speaks to us from another angle once Vlepo enters her mind. Her thought is centered on Tiresias. *And you, old blind fool, what makes you any different from your brothers? Why should we mark you credit for noting the obvious?* (44).

Tiresias thinks that genuine exchange could be better advanced if the men and women could *see* that his wisdom is the bridge to connect arguments from each side of the gender line. But Agave raises questions: "What does the frenzy give to you, Tiresias? . . . What can we women do with *you*?" (46–47). Tiresias, visibly disturbed by the questions, answers that he is a seer. But Agave snaps back at him that "The frenzy gives us all foresight, Tiresias. You are not exceptional here" (47). Agave and the maenads ruffle Tiresias, not to tear him limb from limb, but simply to show him that women can contend with him. As Vlepo finds himself ankle deep in blood while he is in Tiresias's head, we witness the seer's concern: *By the grape-clustered grace of Dionysos, I scream for the reason in passion, and he will not answer me, but sends these Maenads to pound me into memory. I hope for some memory and cry for all those who are remembered by no one, whose names spill like my blood in the soil of this earth* (48–49).

The story of Kadmos that surfaces in *Frenzy* looks to history as foundation. Seconds after Dionysos enters Thebes, Tiresias, the blind prophet, stands outside the palace gate and summons Kadmos to accompany him to Mount Cithareon to get a look at the new god Dionysos. Kadmos replies, "You follow fashion like a hound and so you wear it. This god is no god. He is false, and my grandson, now king, will purge his name from the prayers used in our temple . . . . You had best keep your words couched in mystic jargon, my friend, else you be too clearly comprehended. Do not leave it to me to render your text unintelligible" (5).

Kadmos does not feel that control of and ruling of the kingdom can benefit from mystic jargon and unintelligible text. What clearly is comprehended, he believes, is the sense of history in which a nation is rooted. Hence he does not give credit to Dionysos as a part of that sense of history. He declares Dionysos as false, does not identify him as his grandson, and declares that his other grandson, Pentheus, will purge the name of Dionysos from sacred worship. Kadmos will do whatever he needs to do to secure the kingdom, relinquish power when the hour demands such a move, and take power back when the time is ripe.

When Dionysos sends Vlepo, who has transformed into a louse into the head of Kadmos, Vlepo says, "I saw images and words and sounds, all coming at me in a rush of sensation, which I more than appreciated but experienced in a disturbing fashion and in a manner that defied tearing away my gaze" (25). Here Everett repositions the spotlight to advance framing text not from the pedestal of carnal frenzy, but from the base of exploring the value of collective memory as a sustaining force in human development. Inside the head of Kadmos, Vlepo witnesses the former king surmise, *Pentheus . . . my grandson . . . you stupid young twit . . . you heir to my greatness . . . my king and no king at all . . . . You fight me lamely, youth still nurturing that fatal soft portion of the heart; your failing is, and will be until such time as it is not, that killing in battle is easy and killing at home is difficult* (25).

Kadmos is furious that Pentheus can sway men in battle but cannot make the women caught up in a maddened frenzy return to their homes from the hills of Cithaeron. Kadmos does not feel that the heart of Pentheus will ever serve as guide to secure the kingdom if Pentheus cannot kill what is weak within the state and to give strength to what is strong. Given the blindness of his grandson about the present, Kadmos does not see that Pentheus can contribute to the future. Like Dionysos, who has no past but only versions of stories about the past, Pentheus has the stories but disavows the past. As a louse inside the head of Kadmos, Vlepo is witness to the grave concern that spins in the mind of the former king: *You, Pen-theus, will some day see the foolscap you have worn, and you will grow cruel for the knowledge, you will seek in your waning days to purge the collective memory of this city by replacement* (25–26).

Kadmos wants his grandson Pentheus to round up the women on Cithaeron, beat some sense into them, and drive them home for the good of society. Thus, he admonishes that Pentheus can kill in battle, but he cannot kill the spirit of fire that accounts for the women having aban-doned their homes. Pentheus, of course, is too preoccupied with secur-ing and maintaining imperial power to be concerned about running to Cithaeron to round up some frenzied women. Inside the head of Kadmos, Vlepo allows us to see the old man reflect on his disgust with his grandson:

> *Power kills where power is and knows no love except for itself, but I would not teach you that, nor should you have a son will you teach him. Power is pre-liminary to all things and preontological and puts all other things into their nooks. Power is not infinite for god or man, but neither is it finite . . . . Am I a bad man? Am I a selfish man? There is no malignity or illiberality in a life that seeks and feeds on power. These citizens of mine, good pawns, ushers for a show they do not comprehend, take seats and see all too clearly and impo-tently the mockery I make behind your back, my grandson.* (25–26)

Kadmos muses that the power of the throne must be strengthened. Thus, unlike the other players in his house, he surmises that he must write the script to center on where power has been relinquished. Through the ob-servation of Vlepo inside his head, we see further the position of Kadmos as he reflects on Pentheus. Kadmos muses, *You will hate me as you do now, but deep in your heart you will thank me for a hardness that I never knew in my living. So, in my way I am making you great. I am creating your story, I am giving you history, but know that there are knots of these strings that can never be undone. Pentheus, you stupid young twit, know that there is no such thing as misrule as long as you rule. Bring back the women to my kingdom, away from that intruder who would have them march through one fog into another and out* (26).

We are now clear that all members of the House of Kadmos have been writing their own story to preach their own sermon, which serves to aug-ment frame in *Frenzy* based on *The Bacchae*. But Kadmos does not buy any of these stories, and certainly not Dionysos's version of having entered Thebes as a god to vindicate the honor of his fallen mother while attempting to establish his divinity to forge a new religion. The story that Kadmos writes is the story of Pentheus, the name of his grandson being emblematic of the five senses, the passions that must be balanced to preempt life from being torn limb from limb.

Concerned that Thebes is at an external standstill because of the infighting taking place in his house, Kadmos proffers that *power is preliminary to all things* (25). The prefix *pre* adjoined to the Latin word *liminaris* is ascribed to a threshold, an entrance. To forge an opening through the haze of confusion, Kadmos also reflects that power is preontological. Hence *Frenzy* projects Kadmos as metaphysically structuring an argument not based on an imposter who seeks to establish divinity, but on the existence of divine force manifested in the nature of being. *Ontology* calls to the forefront the question what sort of being can subsist by itself, and what sort is in its very nature dependent on another. To give meaning to their respective life, Dionysos is dependent on the story of Semele; Agave is dependent on the story of her sisters; to lessen conflict, the blind prophet Tiresias is dependent on bridging the stories of the men and the women; and claiming for the good of Thebes, Kadmos sets out to rewrite the entire history of past and present to secure his kingdom's future.

Kadmos is aware that there are those who might think him selfish once his plan to restructure the text is executed. But for him power is neither infinite nor finite. For him power is relative to the executor at the moment of execution. Rather than surrender that moment by allowing Pentheus to go and spy on Dionysus and risk being swayed, Kadmos imprisons Pentheus by restraining him with ropes to his bed. Here *Frenzy* forges an involved climax, different from the ending of Euripides's play when Agave tears her son, Pentheus, limb from limb given her wild intoxication brought on by the vine. Once deceived, twice fooled, Kadmos will not take that chance. He informs that there is no meanness ("illiberality") nor disloyalty nor disaffection ("malignity") expressed by one who seeks power who conceivably wants to be loved as opposed to be feared. Kadmos accepts that desperate times call for desperate measures. By reversing the order of the frame of the story, we are led by Kadmos to believe that he is establishing a historical account that can be sealed for posterity.

Believing that one does not concede power to the powerless, nor that one should support the powerless canceling out each other, Kadmos plays his powerless grandsons against each other. First, he binds Pentheus to his bed with ropes so that eventually his emaciated body dies a slow and agonizing death. Simultaneously, he sends for a third grandson, Actaeon, who, for his daughter Autonoe, "bore a resemblance to Pentheus in size and shape, but the features of his face lacked the same definition" (130). Meanwhile, Vlepo takes us into the head of Kadmos to witness how he reflects on the women, *their chatter and moaning drowning all attempts at discourse* (126). Vlepo then shifts to show how Kadmos reflects on Pentheus: *While in a chamber I detain my grandson, peeking in occasionally to see that his brain is decaying and leaving him a mere case, working to neglect the memory of a boy I once claimed to love, laboring to exculpate actions against my own blood. But I am too far gone, lost down a trail from which I have never strayed, wondering whom I thought I was deluding when I surrendered my crown* (126).

Kadmos sends Actaeon to spy on the maenads. Immediately, he is captured and the maenads think they have cornered a wild beast: "Agave returned to the kill and with the knife made a cut just beneath the skin at the penis, then made a shallow incision down the body to the throat, opening the animal" (152). Inside his home, Kadmos says to Pentheus, "Perhaps you were too smart and good to either rule or serve as a marionette. Regardless: You were a proud disappointment to me" (153–54). While Agave marches with the head of Actaeon on a stick and places it before the city gate, Kadmos saws off the head of Pentheus as three of his lieutenants enter the room. Vlepo witnesses the deed and the thoughts of Kadmos: *At what are they staring? They fear me, and that is good, for I am their tyrant, yes the word is only bad on the tongues of the weak—I am their tyrant. I am a tyrant, a powerful, beautiful, unashamed tyrant. A despot! And they will do well who know the truth. My power reads on me like a film, a dusting, and they will do well who see it* (157).

Now we know the full story. *Frenzy* leaves us standing in a pool of blood because of the violence produced by the clashing of the characters' texts. Even Kadmos has been lying, stringing us along, pretending that he would write a script from a preontological base. Simply, he rewrites the script from the viewpoint of a tyrant, and hence is no better than all others in his house that he accuses of weakness. If we revisit Vlepo as witness at the earlier point where he had gone inside the head of Pentheus, in the end we come away with Pentheus, emblematic of the five senses, as the model that sustains Everett's discourse. His echo topples every other argument. Vlepo thinks that *Meaning is what I seek in this dimension and in some others as well. But what sense is meaning where one's word rules. What advantage can be found in standing alone in the purchased adoration of subjects? I wish Kadmos had chosen to die king* (27).

By narrative's end, we see that Everett's structuring of language in the novel, not the frame of *The Bacchae*, takes center stage in *Frenzy*. Everett is the master architect who has recast *The Bacchae* as frame in order to frame his own text in a cultural continuum that includes African and African American history and the African American literary tradition. *Frenzy* is a story/line cast in the Eternal Present and is centered on a host of characters who embrace the notion that one only has the moment that one has. Each character is preoccupied with limited space. In writing *Frenzy*, Everett shows the reader that the issues presented in the novel are just as relevant to other cultures. Indeed, by writing the novel and by positioning *Frenzy* as a link between Afro-Asiatic cultural history and Greek cultural history, Everett demonstrates that a narrative as seemingly devoid of any connection to black culture is, indeed, tied to it based on the epistemological sentiments the novel interrogates.

When Dionysus enters Thebes with a band of followers, history turns on itself to haunt Thebes. Will Thebes, can Thebes, embrace the story about the mother of this transplant, given that he presents many versions? By drawing on versions of *The Bacchae*, Everett structures *Frenzy* to shows us multiple descriptions of the same struggle under different lights. In "A Nigerian Version of a Greek Classic: Soyinka's Transformation of *The Bacchae*," Norma Bishop observes, "Both Euripides and Soyinka deal with the problem of stale empty ritual traditions, as well as jingoistic attraction to the new. Cadmus and Tiresias represent the inherited wisdom of the elders . . . . Pentheus, on the other hand, is an iconoclast who would rather trust his own wisdom and not accept anything foreign, strange, or undignified" (Bishop 72). Yet each leading character, each character who struggles to lead delivers a respective sermon that constitutes text. Everett reminds us that "Writing is not just the putting of words on paper, but also the getting of the words to a community. A community, not a public" ("Signing to the Blind" 11).

In *Frenzy* Percival Everett gives us a blueprint to distinguish between the two functions of the chronicler of human action. Thus he bequeaths to us a legacy framed in African American and Western literary traditions that hopefully will encourage us to avoid making the same mistake ten times over as we chronicle our own life. And he cautions us:

> Writing is by its very nature subversive. As a disenfranchised people one of the legacies is that the subversion of our writing is political. Even when our work seeks to be something else, it is a reaction to the position in which we and our works have been placed. America sees us, but cannot be displeased. It is as if our culture is waiting outside a collapsed building, sighing with relief each time a dead person turns out to be someone it does not know. But still, someone is dead. ("Signing to the Blind" 11)

As we move to preempt anything or anyone tearing us limb from limb in the future, continually as we attempt to bridge the past, may the Eternal Present counsel what serves as mortal bookmark.

Notes

1. Throughout my paper, the sustained spelling for Dionysos will adhere to the listing in *Frenzy* unless presented differently in quotes from other sources.

2. Percival Everett, *Frenzy*. Subsequent quotes from this text will appear as page numbers in parentheses. The text of the author will be encased in quotation marks; and the text of the character, Vlepo, as manifestation of Dionysos in the role of "mortal bookmark" once he enters the head of another character, will as in the book be italicized.

3. Bowie Duncan, "Jean Toomer's *Cane*: A Modern Black Oracle," assesses *Cane* as a traditional and modern work that exemplifies a bacchic statement. "According to Sir James George Frazer in *The Golden Bough* (1890), particularly in the section 'Dying and Reviving God' and 'Spirits of the Corn and Wild,' peopled with Adonis, Attis, Osiris, and Dionysus who were emblematic of, among other things, the seasons'

and the animal and vegetable kingdoms' growth patterns, primitive man was inherently bound up in the rhythms of an organic life and all its integral variations. Much of man's literature through the ages reflects some perspective of such patterns, and Jean Toomer's *Cane* (1923) is one such example which is at the same time traditional and very modern. Whatever one says about the influence that spawned *Cane*, whether the book is attributed to the English literary tradition Toomer so often elicits, speaking of juju men and the folk soul, or his own experience in Washington or Georgia, the book is informed by a substance, cane, that is the center of things as was Spenser's 'strond' and the ancient's Dionysys. It is this emblem or substance that must be understood to know the message of the oracle" (Duncan 329). Inspired by Duncan's approach, in addition to other works, my dissertation is titled "The *Bacchae* of Jean Toomer."

4. Herodotus (Euterpe—book II/entry 49: 114–15) offers the following commentary about bacchic worship. "Melampus the son of Amytheon, cannot (I think) have been ignorant of this ceremony—nay, he must, I should conceive, have been well acquainted with it. He it was who introduced into Grece the name of Bacchus, the ceremonial of his worship, and the procession of the phallus. He did not, however, so completely apprehend the whole doctrine as to be able to communicate it entirely, but various sages since his time have carried out his teaching to greater perfection. Still it is certain that Melampus introduced the phallus, and that the Greeks learnt from him the ceremonies they now practice. I therefore maintain that Melampus, who was a wise man, and had acquired the art of divination, having become acquainted with the worship of Bacchus through knowledge derived from Egypt, introduced it into Greece, with a few slight changes, at the same time he brought in various other practices. For I can by no means allow that it is by mere coincidence that the Bacchic ceremonies in Greece are so nearly the same as the Egyptians—they would have been more Greek in their character, and less recent in origin. Much less can I admit that the Egyptians borrowed these customs, or any other, from the Greeks. My belief is that Melampus got his knowledge of them from Cadmus the Tyrian, and the followers who he brought from Phoenicia into the country which is now called Boeotia."

5. Context for the concept of the Eternal Present central to analysis in my chapter draws from "The Fourth Stage: Through the Mysteries of Ogun to the Origin of Yoruba Tragedy" in *Myth, Literature and the African World* (1976) by Wole Soyinka. He identifies in keeping with the Fourth Stage an individual's "experience of being and non-being, his dubiousness as essence and matter, intimations of transience and eternity, and the harrowing drives between uniqueness and Oneness." Further context for this idea is gleaned from *The Fourth Way* (1957) by P. D. Ouspensky, which centers on the work of the Armenian mystic Georges Ivanovich Gurdjieff.

Additional focus for the concept is derived from the *I Ching*, the Book of Change central to Chinese philosophy based on the theory that change permeates development because there is permanence, and permanence permeates development because there is change, the ceaseless flow—*ying* and *yang*, governed by extremes balanced: dawn/dusk as the cosmic twins of day and night; east/west as the cosmic twins of south/north; spring/fall as the cosmic twins of summer/winter.

6. Isidore Okpewho states in "Soyinka, Euripides, and the Anxiety of Empire" that this article was being published as a substantially condensed version of a chapter in a forthcoming study titled *Contesting Empire: Black Writers and the Western Canon*. Thus, Okpewho was cautioned against citing any part of the present paper without the author's consent.

Chapter 4

The Preservationist Impulse in Percival Everett's "True Romance"

FRÉDÉRIC DUMAS

Readers may easily relate to the geographical and imaginative landscapes depicted in Percival Everett's 2004 short-story collection, *Damned if I Do*, which, on the whole, are set in locales in the southwestern United States. The story collection displays characters striving to reach an appropriate balance between the wildness of their environment and their largely unsettled lives. With its focus on a lonely hero determined to fight for the preservation of his land in New Mexico and the halcyon lifestyle the landscape would afford him against a planned urban development zone, "True Romance" stands out as the only story in the collection directly concerned with environmental activism.

Everett's poetic universe in "True Romance" and in longer narratives such as *Watershed* (1996), *Grand Canyon, Inc* (2001), *American Desert* (2004), *Wounded* (2005), and *Assumption* (2011) is grounded in an American literary tradition that extols the positive values of nature, particularly those of the West, which has often been endowed with a mythical dimension that paradoxically denies it a tangible existence. This process consists in an

"aestheticization of landscape" through which the American wilderness was transformed, step by step, into "picturesque scenes," an appropriation that "removed it from the realm of nature and designated it a legitimate object of artistic consumption." [. . .] During the first part of the twentieth century, that aestheticization, which left a legacy of unreality, happened roundly around the West, a region where "nature's text" would have to wait awhile before many would learn to read it "as something other than fiction." (Johnson 220)

The allusion to "romance" in the title orients the reception of the narrative in the context of a celebrated trend that includes masterpieces such as Hawthorne's *House of the Seven Gables* (1850) and whose conventions are kept very much alive in contemporary literature that employs magic realism as an aesthetic device. The oxymoronic juxtaposition displayed in the expression "True Romance" draws attention to the conflicting relation between reality and its literary expression; it proves all the more telling since Rawley Tucker, the autodiegetic narrator, is to embark on a one-man preservationist crusade raising contradictory issues, notably between his romantic vision of nature and his burgeoning apprehension of the inherent financial realities of the encroachment of big business. Such contradictions lie at the heart of the founding of America, which was oriented toward the recovery of the Garden of Eden and yet was sustained by an irrepressible urge to acquire land that led to genocide, slavery, and the advent of monopolistic capitalism. For historical reasons, the utopian impulse survived the physical confrontation with the American environment:

Nature not just in America but *as* America was a dream from the beginning. An unoccupied continent plus the young republic's good fortune for having its "fathers" men of the enlightenment combined—as is written in the Declaration of Independence—to give authority to "the laws of nature and to Nature's God." (Kazin 7)

American literature continues to probe the essence of an American nature in a fairly obsessive manner. In so doing, it is instrumental in shaping nature as a fantasy and keeping the natural environment at the heart of the concept. Nature writing is a crucial facet of the writing of America, and "True Romance" may be said to constitute the cornerstone of Everett's ecological writing. It is in tune with the overall optimistic spirit of *Damned if I Do*, which oscillates between the two poles of the famed American "pastoral impulse"—*viz.*, regression and vitality.

I will begin by analyzing Rawley's critical yet qualified approach to mercantilism in American society. His anachronistic lifestyle will appear only superficially regressive because, in reality, it stems from a strong system of values that he believes, in an environmentalist/preservationist American tradition, is worth fighting for; "True Romance" puts forward a doctrine of environmental activism that turns out to involve not only the question of the end and the means to achieve it, but also mostly that of the paradoxical price of utopia.

The Pastoral Impulse and the Business Question

"True Romance" remarkably fits the concept of the pastoral impulse put forward by Leo Marx in his groundbreaking *Machine in the Garden* (1964) and refined in *The Pilot and the Passenger* (1988). After holding all sorts of jobs in many places, dissatisfied with his literary career and the direction of his life, Rawley Tucker has been ironically leading the life of a lonely romance writer. His retreat to the mountains outside Taos is a characteristic move of an American writer who seeks a pastoral impulse for inspiration and insight:

> A notable feature about imaginative literature in America, when viewed from an ecological perspective, is the number of our most admired works in obedience to a pastoral impulse. By "pastoral impulse" I mean the urge in face of society's increasing power and complexity, to retreat in the direction of nature. The most obvious form taken by this withdrawal from the world of established institutions is a movement in space. The writer or narrator describes, or a character enacts, a move away from a relatively sophisticated to a simpler, more "natural environment [. . .]: it is a landscape that bears fewer marks of human intervention. (*Pilot* 151–52)

Rawley, in his desire for this pastoral impulse, echoes the sentiments of Daniel Boone when he says, "I lamented the fact that too many people already knew where I lived" (66). In desperate need of elbow room, he selects and purchases his property to avoid human interaction and chooses to relate only with a few selected individuals. He demonstrates his desire to be left alone during his conversation with the owner of the local fishing store about the question of urbanized landscape. He reveals his reason for purchasing his land: "I told him I couldn't find a place to fish the Battenkill where I couldn't see a house or a road" (63).

The Narrator's anachronistic lifestyle seemingly likens him to a devotee of the past. Modern technology, Rawley believes, has contributed to his failure to become the writer he desires to be. Using a typewriter or a word processor, for instance, denotes his failure at literary creation. He says, "I sat down to write, or at least *type*, some more of my latest, ever-more-like-the-last-one, piece-of-crap novel" (66). He distrusts other technology as well, such as graphite fishing gear, which also represent modernity and mercantilism. Instead, he prefers his "turn-of-the-century Abercrombie and Fitch bamboo rod" (63) and cultivates a self-reliance that prompts him to refuse friendly offers of rides when he walks home from the store with his groceries. The only technological possession he truly values is his decrepit truck, which turns out to be pivotal in the unfolding of the plot, as well as an ideological catalyst for the decisions he makes concerning his land.

Just like its owner, the jalopy tends to follow its independent course and functions properly only in nonurban environments: "The problem with the old Jeep was that you had to be sure to park on a hill if you wanted to start it again. [. . .] I was okay at my place on the mountain, but when I drove down to Taos, I was in trouble" (61). The broken-down starter, however, merely seems to impose its will upon Rawley, whose ingenuity is constantly put to the test, guaranteeing that man truly masters his machine.

Rawley's stubborn attachment to the undependable truck borders on the sentimental and goes against "the dominant American ideology of material progress" (*Machine* 379). Yet it denotes an underlying celebration of Americanness, through the values the truck is made to symbolize. Universally identified as a quintessential American icon, a Jeep stands for the archetype of the sturdy automobile, whose strictly utilitarian purpose perfectly agrees with American pragmatism. Letting his friend, the Chicken Lady (who happens to be a man), "tell great lies about its history to Texans and Oklahomans who romanticized such relics" (61) endows the Jeep with a mythical aura that makes it a quintessential part of the essence of the place, the environment.

The truck thus tells a great deal about its owner's value system, as well as those of its bard, the Chicken Lady, who praises its value and whose personality and attitude, in turn, reflects these values. For, strangely enough, the Chicken Lady pretends to be the owner of the Jeep: "I allowed him to put a FOR SALE sign on the windshield of my truck. He loved to dicker about price" (61). What Everett demonstrates here is that Rawley and the Chicken Lady are ideologically similar when it comes to money and property. The poultry dealer's relation with money is not based on the desire for things; his sense of the value of the self is not contingent upon acquisition, unlike the developers who are interested in purchasing Rawley's land. For instance, at the end of the story, he produces a five-dollar bill from his pocket which he unhesitatingly gives to Rawley at the end of the story as payment for the truck. The Chicken Lady does not understand the concept of wealth. Even though it's only five dollars, "'The Chicken Lady doesn't understand how there can be that much money in one person's pocket'" (72). Not concerned with profit, his commercial pitch to the Hollywood agents interested in purchasing the truck merely mythologizes the truck for him. The opportunity to sell the truck to the Hollywood agents becomes, for the Chicken Lady, the opportunity for story making. As a storyteller, the Chicken Lady becomes Rawley's counterpart and sheds light on the latter's approach to financial matters. Such disinterestedness in money comes in sharp contrast with the predatory practices of big business, represented in the story by the Hollywood producer who wants to buy the truck for an inordinate sum and whose presence is symbolized in the narrative by the "circling hawk" (72) hovering above Rawley and his fishing partner. The Jeep proves a vehicle, as it were, for an individualistic lifestyle miles away from the selfish reality of an essentially business-related America epitomized by the automobile industry.[1] The Chicken Lady's mercantilism is a parody of entrepreneurship, a mere alibi for establishing friendly communication with strangers; his physical appearance makes him a Groucho Marx–like businessman wearing "Black Red Wings with one loose sole" (76) and "holding a big black rooster under one arm" (62). The "unlit cigar in his free hand" (62) completes the lampoon of the archetypal cigar-smoking greedy capitalist and denotes his lack of aggressiveness during the business transaction. This description is all the more ironic since his name also happens to be that of his poultry business. As a "chicken" and a "lady," this makes him a most unlikely embodiment of greed and profit-making impulses exemplified by the Hollywood producers.

Despite his slightly grotesque figure and beyond his impressive weight, the Chicken Lady is made to appear as a truly "big man" (62). Unbeknown to the Hollywood producers, his lack of business acumen is more than largely compensated by his affection for and his connection to his fellow human beings. His personality also reveals his love for animals, which he treats with equal respect, as if they were human: "'He's upset today.' The Chicken Lady put a finger on the bird's beak. 'His friend died and he's lonely. So, I'm his company'" (66). Rawley has a comparable attitude toward his animals, and he talks to his cat and his dog as he would to children: "Spoiled rotten, both of you" (66). Through the harmonious combination of two radically opposed personalities—the Chicken Lady's sociability and the narrator's misanthropy—"True Romance" presents the vignette of an ideal community held together by a respect for nature and the environment sustained by an anachronistic American worldview. In a sense, Rawley and the Chicken Lady exhibit attitudes toward nature in the manner of American transcendentalists such as Henry David Thoreau.

A Doctrine of Action

The narrator's property is unpretentious; far from the nearest neighbors, it lies in the midst of a landscape that appears untouched. Rawley lives in harmony with his wild surroundings, which he seems to venerate. Though an avid angler, one of his favorite places is "a section of stream I never fished because it was just too pretty" (70); in the stream is a couple of trout he has been watching for two years without attempting to catch. His respect for the fish and the environment they live in demonstrates his reverence for nature. This part of the stream with its Eden-like characteristics, however, proves most fragile and is endangered by those who would exploit it for monetary gain: "The spot was well above a sharp bend in the flow where the real pot growers in the canyon had repeatedly dammed the creek to divert the water to their crops" (70). In this regard, the pot growers are no different from the movie producers in their eagerness to exploit the surrounding environment. Rawley understands this all too well and decides to take action against encroachment upon his "Eden."

Rawley's lifestyle is not merely contemplative, as one might say about Henry David Thoreau; indeed, when the integrity of his ideal landscape becomes threatened, he overcomes his apprehensiveness and takes, in direct opposition to his identity and image as a writer of romance novels, radical action:

> For a while I was riding up daily to check the stream and destroy their handiwork. After finding a couple of big fish dead below the dam, I got mad and camped out with my shotgun. [. . .] I fired above them, three shells, then I [. . .] fired three more [. . .]. I slept there three nights in a row and they never came back. (70–71)

His resolute attitude is enough to scare the pot growers away and to thwart the pollution caused by the illegal practice. Yet the small-scale defilement of nature resulting from the underground economy proves much less of a threat than the permanent transformation of landscape brought about by the violent intrusion of organized capitalism:

> "They're blasting open a malachite mine up mountain. Jobs. People. Wal-Mart."
> "McDonald's, motels, more people," I said. (73)

The pot growers' dam can be made to disappear without irreparable damage, but the legally planned industrial and commercial development heralds an urban sprawl that will devastate the entire region's ecosystem. The Wal-Mart sign incidentally spotted by Rawley is the symbolic irruption of the "machine in the garden" in his Eden, shattering his "epiphany"—*viz.*, his "feeling of transcendent harmony with his surroundings" (*Machine* 378). The above dialogue between him and his fishing partner voices the dilemma over whether to accept the evils of modernity as ineluctable or resolve to fight its destructive impact on the environment. This universal quandary[2] is felt all the more acutely in the United States, given the unprecedentedly rapid transformation of its landscape:

As cities proliferated and land in the West (much of it owned and sequestered by the Federal government) became less available to the public, land turned into an icon for many Americans increasingly disturbed by the monopoly in every field. (Kazin 115)

In his day, Henry David Thoreau was ambivalent toward the intrusion of the train in the vicinity of Walden Pond. He both praised the advancement of commerce it allowed and denounced its corrupting influence: "trade curses everything it handles; and though you trade in messages from heaven, the whole curse of trade attaches to the business" (Thoreau 52). As a writer he was both fascinated by the industrial creation he mythologized and repelled by the evils of the mass market it contributed to building up: "up come the books, but down goes the wit that writes them" (Thoreau 82).

As for Rawley, he never doubts that the building project he is fighting against will have only destructive effects. Feeling cornered, his instinctive reaction is literally and symbolically to immerse himself in and become one with the now-endangered Enrico Creek: "I reached down beside me and picked up one of my wading boots. I held it to my nose and inhaled the sour smell of the river water that had soaked the felt sole" (73–74). Despite its comic and pathetic aspect, the narrator's immersion in the smelly water of his boots is akin to a secular baptism from which he is reborn as a new man. Humorous though it is, this mystical experience will henceforth, in his mind, legitimize his subsequent actions. His thought process is left to the reader's imagination in the space of the narrative gap that immediately follows. The next paragraph opens *in medias res*, as Rawley is deftly accepting the prodigal offer of the Hollywood executive he had previously turned down—three hundred fifty thousand dollars for renting his mountain abode as a shooting location. As for the truck, he will sell it to the Chicken Lady for a symbolic five dollars so that the latter may make a hefty profit in selling it to the production company. Rawley advises him to "'Hold out for thirty thousand. Okay?'" (77) The sum previously agreed on with the Hollywood executive being twenty-five thousand, Rawley shows even more business savvy when it comes to protecting his friend's interest.

A Paradoxical Utopia

After concluding the lucrative deal with the movie studio executives, Rawley reveals his first course of action: "I [. . .] called a real estate agent, told him I wanted a list of all the pieces of property for sale in and around Enrico. Tomorrow, I would go the county's office and find out who owned what. I would buy all I could, where I could, and get in the way of any development" (75). Rawley's decision to acquire the land in order to keep it free from man's encroaching presence will turn it into a sanctuary, sheltered for its own sake. Doing so, he behaves as a true preservationist:

> Preservationism is the desire to protect parts of the natural world from human change and development. A modern term for a general movement that arose in industrialized countries after 1860, it is often opposed to conservation—the concept of scientific, sustainable resource use.[3]

Rawley's action is not political insofar as it does not proceed from collective dialogue; instead, it appears motivated mostly by his private designs. Though it will bear great consequence on the whole community, his decision is totally individualistic. It consists in using the beneficial aspects of the very system that jeopardizes his environment. Greedy acquisition of land, which proved instrumental in the advent of such flagships of big business as train companies and mining corporations, assigned monetary value to what had heretofore been freely enjoyed by all. Free enterprise transformed American land into real estate, with mostly harmful ecological consequences. Rawley's metamorphosis into an environmentally friendly imperialistic landowner suggests that the same financially based processes that led to the deterioration of nature may also be used to save it.

Paradoxically, then, the narrator's massive purchase partakes of the greed traditionally associated with monopolistic wildcat capitalism and goes against a progressive trend of American environmentalism that dates back from the nineteenth century. Henry George, the economist and politician whose idea of a "single tax" in the 1860s promised the advent of a utopian approach to wealth and landownership, had a wholly different vision in mind. Alfred Kazin points out that "George's reverence for the land as primary source of wealth, the inherent property of the community, led to the fervent conviction (and fond illusion) that no one really needs more land than he can use" (116). Rawley's plan to buy as much land as possible, without any other justification than his own individualistic creed, appears as a way to achieve one man's utopia, independently of the community's interest.

The two conflicting trends in the capitalist logic he adopts happen to echo those at work in preservationism itself, which perforce positions humans as radically distinct from the wildlife they aim at protecting on the grounds of a common nature. For all its disinterestedness, the acquisition of land is yet another symptom of the European-American's drive to possess:

> The injunction of preservationism is to disconnect ourselves from wilderness in order to save it, and the reason we must save it is the depth of our connection to it. Its features "seem indelibly etched in our psyches" [. . .] without it "we might not reach our potential or maintain our identity." We crave what we want to save from ourselves. For our preservation-minded forebears a century ago, that approach/avoid predicament was becoming tragically ironic, and its irony involved other ironies and like conundrums, all of which came into play in a story of increasing etherealization. Conventional in American preservationist literature is the distinction between preservation and use, but, of course [. . .] preservation also means use of a kind. [. . .] "it was not for the sake of the creatures themselves, but for the sake of men, that birds and animals would be protected in sanctuaries and wild-life parks." (Johnson 219)

Rawley never states his ultimate intention; his plans for the land remain undisclosed. His aggressive purchasing tactics are akin to those of nineteenth-century robber barons such as J. P Morgan, John Rockefeller, and Cornelius Vanderbilt; selling his truck to the Chicken Lady for virtually nothing, however, seems to preclude the possibility of his sudden transformation into a greedy capitalist. Ironically, money will enable him to transform his surrounding environment by maintaining it as it already is.

Though Rawley greatly limits his contact with the urban world, he never shows a wholesale rejection of modernity and should not be considered a primitivist. He notes, "But the town was there and it had a grocery market better than the convenience store in Questa. It also offered a fly-fishing shop and I guess I owed a thank you to yuppies and the Orvis catalog for that" (62). His is a qualified attitude to change; though he shows interest in newness he remains sensually attracted to manufactured products made with natural material: "on my bimonthly visits, I'd stop in and shake the expensive graphite rods and run my fingers along the even more expensive bamboo sticks" (62).

Just as Rawley's neighbors interpret his unusual isolation as a rich man's whim, his rustic lifestyle is taken over by the economic system that, being based on supply and demand, equates his discriminating taste with luxury. Such reactions are based on misunderstanding; neither a primitivist nor a countrified yuppie, Rawley opts for a balanced approach to the inevitable interaction between nature and civilization, which places him in the pastoral tradition. As Leo Marx advances:

> To be clear about the significance of pastoralism in the American context, [. . .] it should not be thought of as the logical antithesis of the modern belief in progress. That hypothetical role belongs to primitivism, the doctrine which holds that the environment most conducive to well-being is the purest, least developed state of nature. The ideal situation that a true primitivist may be supposed to cherish is located as far away as possible, in space or time or both, from the urban centers of advanced civilization. The pastoral world-view, on the other hand, comes into focus somewhere between the logical extremes of the primitivist and the progressivist views of change—of history. [. . .] The pastoralist's viewpoint entails neither an uncritical embrace of material progress nor its total repudiation. (*Pilot* 187)

A primitivist would completely shun mercantilist relationships, which is precisely what Rawley pretended to do before his preservationist resolution. Before coming up with his solution he thinks, "'I don't want to do business with people I don't like anymore.' Which was a lie, because I pretty much hated my publisher, my editor, and my agent" (73). In Rawley's pastoral universe, financial independence is the key to living out one's principles:

"You're refusing nearly a hundred thousand dollars?" [. . .]
"Yes, [. . .] I'm happy. I don't need the money." (69)

Amusingly and revealingly, when finally resolving to strike the deal with the Hollywood agent, he finds himself in the same situation as his reluctant mare, to which he is administering worming medicine. At that very moment he is conversing with the producer who is holding the mare's harness. Rawley tells him, "'She hates this stuff [. . .] but we're done'" (74). Similarly, though Rawley's radical concessions with the business world are figuratively hard to swallow, they are necessary to secure the life he longs for; they might even ultimately guarantee his survival. Protection of the land, Rawley believes, will enable him to live a more stress-free, tranquil life. His mercantilist/preservationist compromise links him to one of America's most famous preservationists.

The creation of one of America's illustrious national parks illustrates the ambivalent approach Muir took when it came to making use of the land he was supposed to protect from encroaching civilization:

Muir, who thought of the Garden of Eden as a prototype for Yosemite, operated his sawmill there to manufacture "lumber for tourist development." There was "a dark side" to the artifice of idolized wilderness—after all, "Muir's temple was bloodied from the start by the violent eviction of the native Indians"—and always the eventuality that wilderness would turn out to be "not 'wholly other' but 'wholly us.'"[4]

Hence, from the American preservationist movement's beginning, the maintenance of wilderness required management, especially in the West. Such management is what New Mexico nature writer and scientist Sharman Apt Russell has acknowledged as "an oxymoron we all have to live with" (Johnson 220).

Utopian environmentalism aims at preserving nature in its pristine state, yet that unspoiled quality is necessarily an artifact. In "True Romance" Rawley takes the ensuing oxymoronic combination of money and ideal for granted. Limiting his narration to action and dialogue denotes his refusal to back up his aspirations with any ideological discourse. He is clearly anti-doctrinaire when he says, "I catch and release as much as the next guy, but I despise religions of all kinds" (64). His thoughts constitute an oblique reference to his lifestyle, which he is ready to fight for without falling into extremes of proselytism.

Conclusion

Borrowing from a well-established American literary tradition contributes to legitimizing the ecological creed of Percival Everett's "True Romance." The timely appearance of the Hollywood agent partakes of a narrative device commonly used in countless popular romances based on the Horatio Alger pattern, in which a deserving hero overcomes adversity and achieves social success with the providential help of a wealthy father figure. Such tales hardly ever question the positive nature of capitalism. The subversiveness of "True Romance" does not lie merely in the dissident preservationist message, but in its formal expression. Just as Daniel Barkley, the African American guitarist in Everett's allegorical "The Appropriation of Cultures," eventually manages to defeat white racism in South Carolina by playing the *a priori* conservative and racist "Dixie" as a jazz piece and then by adopting the Confederate flag without any trace of irony, Everett resorts to a conformist literary vector for his hero's nonconformist standards.

Rawley's instinctive quest for a virginal landscape bears traces of the archetypal desire to recover the feminine matrix.[5] In this regard, he is the descendant of a prestigious American line of writers and thinkers "like Irving, Cooper, and Simms [who] [. . .] converted the pastoral possibility into the exclusive prerogative of a single male figure, living out a highly eroticized and intimate relationship with a landscape at once suggestively sexual, but overwhelmingly maternal" (Kolodny 134). Caught between their life-oriented erotic impulse and the death-wish denoted by a symbolic recapture of the womb, these writers' literary heroes express an existential predicament with social import:

> There is an undeniable element of escapism about this familiar, perhaps universal, desire to get away from the imperatives of a complicated social life. [. . .] if our literary pastoralism lent expression only to this escapist impulse, we would be compelled to call it self-indulgent, puerile,

or regressive. But fortunately this is not the case. In most American pastorals the movement toward nature also may be understood as a serious criticism, explicit or implied, of the established social order. It calls into question a society dominated by a mechanistic system of value, keyed to perfecting the routine means of existence, yet oblivious to its meaning and purpose. (*Pilot* 152)

In Everett's subtle approach, Rawley is not presented as an altruist. Yet individualism being historically associated with the national spirit, his preservationist creed is to be felt as working for the public good. His legalistic approach to the destruction of the environment affirms the soundness of the national institutions.

"True Romance" aptly illustrates the ironic title of the short story collection. *Damned if I Do* inevitably brings to mind its unwritten corollary "damned if I don't," asserting the futility of making choices. Such an interpretation, however, runs contrary to the renowned American faith in individualistic willpower, which may—or not—be thought to sustain Rawley's enterprise. The narrator's choice of action, then, may also be considered as a metaphor of the writing-reading process. Lance—Rawley's pen name as a free-*lance* romance novelist—is seen to literally embody the values he stands for; this move, however, reaches beyond the literary question and positions him as a "free Lance." His status as a hack writer makes him the negative counterpart of the empirical author and brings to the fore the question of writing as social commitment.

Notes

1. Three stories of the collection that follow on from one another include the potent presence of a truck. At the very end of "Warm and Nicely Buried," Lem seems to have acquired a life of its own: "His truck bounced wildly along the wagon-rutted lane even though he was driving slowly" (127). The truck's "wild" behavior is rendered logical by Lem's partner's humorous statement, as he strews the floor with piñon shells: "'This is natural, bio-stuff. No need to clean these up. They'll break down naturally and contribute to the ecosystem, which is your car'" (126). Just as in "True Romance," the truck is closely related to its natural environment, with which it merges in unexpected fashion. David's truck in "The Appropriation of Cultures"

eventually becomes the wedge that brings down southern white racism as the new, black owner turns inside out the symbolic value of the "rebel-flag decal covering the rear window" (96). A great part of the action of the following "Afraid of the Dark" also revolves around a truck, carrying a black and white stallion whose panicky reaction to darkness turns out to shed light on the unconscious roots of racism. In each case, the truck acts as a revealer of fundamental American characteristics.

2. "This is not just an American problem [. . .] there were once great pine and cedar forests in Mesopotamia and Lebanon, which Sumerians and Semites plundered for their great public building; Crete was deforested by the Minoans 3,500 years ago; first Greece and then Rome ravaged the whole northern coast of the Mediterranean for their naval fleets and building projects. To this day, the bleaching bones of the Greek mountains testify to the severity of the landscape degradation accomplished by the supposed originary paragons of Western civilization. [. . .] Whatever the ideology or mythic shape all these peoples gave their actions, the result was devastation of the land, changes in weather and rainfall, and widespread extinction of wildlife" (Westling 169).

3. "Preservationism," *Encyclopedia of World Environmental History*, ed. Shepard Krech, John Robert McNeill, and Carolyn Merchant (New York: Routledge, 2004), 1018.

4. Despite such incriminations Muir's mythical status in the United States endures, even among contemporary ecocritics: "Muir, when he came face to face with the sublime, was able to articulate the movement in his thinking from Christian anthropocentrism to biocentric pantheism. [. . .] I became so inspired by Muir's writing that I spent three weeks one summer hiking the 210-mile John Muir Trail" (Scheese 1995, 61).

5. "Feminine fecundity has a cosmic model—that of Terra Mater, the universal Genetrix" (Eliade 1968, 144).

Chapter 5

The Mind-Body Split in *American Desert*

Synthesizing Everett's Critique of Race, Religion, and Science

RICHARD SCHUR

At least since Descartes wrote "I think therefore I am," Western philosophy has explored the mind-body problem. The relationship of the mind and the body presents the challenge of distinguishing between the world of ideas and the material forms of existence. In his famous account, Descartes severs the link between the mind and the body to elevate the role of philosophy and reflection in the construction of knowledge. Descartes famously posited: "Although the entire mind seems to be united to the entire body, nevertheless, were a foot or an arm or any other bodily part to be amputated, I know that nothing has been taken away from the mind on that account" (101). Percival Everett has frequently examined philosophical notions in his writing and has long been interested in philosophical questions (Masiki 34). In *American Desert*, he challenges Descartes's theories about the mind-body split and rejects commonsense wisdom about the body. Readers familiar with his oeuvre would likely identify both race and religion as some of Everett's favorite targets for satire. This essay argues that Everett's critique of race and religion are fused in *American Desert* through his deconstruction of the mind-body split. Ultimately, *American Desert* asks what it means to live and live well in a society in which key elements of identity and spirituality pit the mind against the body.

While the mind-body split has been a central concern of Western philosophy, the various traditions of African American cultural and literary critique have tended to frame this problem around the preoccupation with, surveillance over, and ongoing degradation of black bodies. Even though writers from earlier generations rarely framed this issue under the rubric of the mind-body split, this question underpins the freedom narratives, the philosophical and ideological differences between Du Bois and Washington, and arguments among the participants in the Harlem Renaissance; debates among writers of the black arts movement frequently pivoted around the question of how to represent African American bodies and how best to reveal the internal mental processes of African Americans living in a racist and racialized culture. In the early 1970s, Charles Johnson, both an author and a philosopher, sought to develop a phenomenological account of the black body through the lens of Descartes's mind-body split. He makes a number of revealing observations: (1) "The issue at stake is how blacks experience their own bodies within a world of racial restriction"; (2) "I *am* my body while I am also *not* my body"; and (3) "I am conscious of the world through the medium of my body" (254–55). Johnson's account, rendered in a more literary form in *The Oxherding Tale* (1982) and *Dreamer* (1998), reveals the clear gap between a person's body and his or her mind.

In late 1989, Trey Ellis articulated a new vision for African American cultural workers/producers, which he called "the New Black Aesthetic." The aim of this new vision was to eschew essentialist paradigms that Ellis felt had greatly restricted African American artistic production. For Ellis, this New Black Aesthetic, or NBA, "shamelessly borrows and reassembles across both race and class lines" (234). After his first few novels, much of Percival Everett's work came to exemplify the cultural fusion celebrated by Trey Ellis; he rejected naturalist, realist, and black arts approaches to African American literary production and rather embraced such a wide range of Euro-American and African American influences, allusions, and narrative voices that one would be hard pressed to claim that Everett fully embraced Trey Ellis's aesthetic and ideological tenets. Frequently drawing on European philosophy, literary and cultural theory, modernist and postmodernist aesthetics, genre writing, and other influences, Everett developed a style that sampled from numerous traditions, layered symbol upon symbol, relied on frequent breaks or ruptures within his texts, and adopted a much more ironic voice (Schur 216). Much of the irony one discovers in his texts surrounds the notion of the mind-body split.

A number of other contemporary African American writers have further explored the representation of black bodies and considered the mind-body problem from the perspective of the post–civil rights era. From Danzy Sen-na's *Caucasia* (1998), which considers racial passing by a biracial girl, to Paul Beatty's *White Boy Shuffle* (1996), in which the young African Ameri-can male protagonist struggles against racial stereotypes that get mapped onto his basketball-player body and his street-poet mind, recent African American novels explore the continuing legacy of this epistemological conflict. Despite the promise of the post–civil rights era, the black body remains an object of considerable fascination in (white) American cul-ture and many novelists contrast this objectification and reification of the black body against the continuing struggle to de-colonize black minds. Two recent edited collections, Carol Henderson's *America and the Black Body* (2009) and Meri Nana-Ama Danquah's *The Black Body* (2009), explore the contemporary significance of the black body and the ongoing chal-lenge to advance better and fuller representations of it. The debate about the representations of African Americans continues despite the promise of Barack Obama's election and the recent proclamations that the United States has entered a "post-racial" moment.

Even though he has tended to downplay the relevance of his own race to his fiction, Everett has regularly returned to mining the fictional pos-sibilities of the mind-body split in his work, regardless of the race of the characters (Kincaid 378; Masiki 38; and Stewart 303, 306). For instance, in *Zulus* (1990), Everett tells the story of a 300-pound white woman, Al-ice Achitophel, who lives in a post-apocalyptic world where women are no longer fertile. Once she is raped and becomes pregnant, Alice seeks to escape the dominant society and becomes a rebel. The rebels, however, only want her body for breeding purposes when they find out that she is presumably the last fertile woman in existence. In a bizarre turn of events, Alice miraculously begins to grow even larger to the point where she liter-ally explodes, splits from her 300-pound body, and emerges as a more at-tractive and slender woman. However, the shell of Alice's fat body remains in rebel hands, even as she roams freely in her new slender body. Moreover, the thin Alice can *psychically* sense what the fat Alice's discarded head per-ceives as it lies supine in the middle of the rebel camp (*Zulus* 181–83).

Everett's *Glyph* (1999) tells the story of an African American toddler and boy-genius named Ralph. Jacqueline Berben-Masi argues that "*Glyph* ends with an adult mind still imprisoned in a child's body" (227). The entire tone and flow of the novel follows from the incongruity or gap between Ralph's mind and body. The novel does, however, end with Ralph "living peacefully" and seemingly coming to terms with the apparent incongruity (207). Both *Erasure* (2001) and *I Am Not Sidney Poitier* (2009) also explore the consequences when bodies frustrate social expectations and the resulting psychic effects for the "owner" of that body. *Erasure* examines the consequences of the mind-body split in African American literature, while *I Am Not Sidney Poitier* engages in a similar exploration in terms of film and visual culture (Sanchex-Arce 150). What are readers to make of Everett's frequent exploration of this gap between minds and bodies, especially when he refuses to accept the often burdensome label of being a black or African American writer?

While he has clearly explored the mind-body split in other places, *American Desert* takes up this classical philosophical dilemma as the starting point for the novel. In fact, *American Desert* could be profitably read as a postmodern allegory about the perils of abstract identities that are almost completely socially constructed and distinct from actual lived experience. The novel organizes this allegory into three sections with Book One, introducing the philosophical dilemma in its popular—as represented by the media fascination with the novel's main character—and scientific forms. Book Two considers how religion, albeit a fairly fringe version of Christianity, responds to the problem. And Book Three delineates how the government might imagine a world where bodies and minds actually could be split apart. The novel is concluded with Book Four as the protagonist reflects upon his adventures as a mind without a "normally" functioning body and his subsequent decision to end his "life."

The opening lines of the novel emphasize irony and the relationship between consciousness and physical being:

That Theodore Street was dead was not a matter open to debate. The irony of his accidental death went unobserved as no one knew that Theodore was on his way to commit suicide when he was, shall we say interrupted. Now the irony is lost amid the confusion created by Ted's death, departure, demise, dissolution[1] and further by the fact that Ted chooses to relate his own story in third person, an unusual (the occasional politician and athlete aside), but acceptable device, given that, in

a most profound way, he stood—or even—outside himself, not so much
of on the parapet of consciousness but of life itself. (3)

On the following page, the reader learns that the automobile accident that
results in Street's death severed his head from his body but did not leave
a scratch (4). When his wife, Gloria, visits the morgue after the accident,
the narrative emphasizes that she viewed "his head on a video monitor as
it sat in a metal bowl," but that she never identifies the body (5).

Through these opening scenes, Percival Everett elaborates upon Descartes's founding fiction of modern philosophy and transforms it into
the jumping off point for his exploration of the meaning of life in a postmodern world. The narration adopts the language of alienation to describe the comic results of Street's failed suicide attempt. By switching
to what appears as a third-person narrator, Street's own language reveals
how his mind disavows his body and its story. Moreover, his wife can only
recognize his head—not his body—as American culture has rejected the
body and the physical in favor of more abstract forms of identity and
knowledge.

Unlike Descartes (and much philosophical discourse), who narrates this
split romantically, hoping that the mind can triumph over the body, Everett finds comedy in the seemingly endless war between the mind and the
body.[2] It is the failure to reintegrate the two and the resulting failure of social, political, and religious communities that *American Desert* explores. Everett is clearly playing with the relationships among the body, philosophy,
and religion in his comic conversation between a body shared by the heads
of Paul Althaus and Karl Heim and a head shared by two bodies wearing
Heidegger and Hegel tee-shirts, respectively (50). This odd blend of bodies and heads clearly parodies the concepts of transcendence, synthesis,
and separation for which these scholars were known. Everett takes their
metaphors and transforms them into literal philosophical and religious
"truth." Adding to the irony of the mind-body split throughout the novel,
Everett omits any description of Ted Street's race, thereby definitively severing his character's identity, based on racial markers, from his (imagined)
body.

Three days following his decapitation, the family holds his funeral "at a
church Ted never attended when alive" (7). The narration does not identify

the church in overt racial terms, but the novel hints that it might be an African American church. Adding to the irony of what is supposed to be a somber occasion, at the funeral the choir is dressed in "powder blue robes" and the minister, Larville Staige, is wearing a maroon robe (8). The minister frequently relies on the terms "brothers" and "sisters" in his eulogy in direct contrast to Ted's department chair who comes to speak on his behalf (9). Perhaps echoing the stereotypical image of a southern black church from the civil rights movement Staige cools himself with a fan that just happens to feature an image of Martin Luther King (8). The choir supplies a number of loud "amens" and offers a "harmonious hum" before, shockingly, Ted comes back to life (11). While it is not entirely clear if this is in fact an African American church, one could come to this conclusion. However, the fact that Everett renders the scene so racially ambiguous, plays into his aesthetic and political vision of not allowing readers to make assumptions and determinations about Ted based on race.

Still, the very physicality of the church is pitted against Street's failure as an academic and intellectual. Street's decision, in part, stems from his failure to obtain tenure at his university; his manuscript is rejected by an academic press for being too similar to other books. Moreover, before his "death" Street, who is married, had placed his personal and professional life in peril by succumbing to suppressed physical desires through the sexual advances of one of his graduate students, Inga. After he realizes that he will be denied tenure, he meets his replacement, a young, up-and-coming female scholar who has already "published a book on *Beowulf*, but was on the cutting edge of digital imaging of manuscripts" (8). At his funeral, Orville Orson, Street's department chair, eulogized him for the physical work of teaching while implying that he was a failure as an intellectual and a scholar (10–11). Beside the comedy inherent in this funeral scene dominated by academic politics, Everett sets the stage to portray Street as a failed intellect because his body held his mind back. The allusion to a digital version of *Beowulf* represents a literal and symbolic severing of this very visceral epic poem (the written text as body), filled with heroic tales, and its heroic action into just another text in cyberspace (the text as "mind"). It also completes the trajectory of *Beowulf* in its journey from being considered history, then a myth, and now just another hypertext in cyberspace. Again, in this scene, Everett interrogates Descartes's notion of the mind-body split. Everett sustains his interrogation through Ted's "death" and his miraculous "rebirth" during his funeral.

In the middle of this absurd funeral, Ted Street—in a clear and ironic repetition of Jesus' resurrection—rises from his casket. Because the mortician stole his pants, Street "was naked from the waist down, his tallywacker hanging rather handsomely out in front of him" (11). Not unsurprisingly, "Ted's resurrection caused a stir, a terrible riot which spread from the church and into the streets" (16). In his retelling of this foundational moment of Christianity, Everett transforms the miraculous nature of the resurrection into a postmodern comedy that does not inspire spirituality but violence and chaos. Nevertheless, Ted's "rebirth" renders startling physical and psychological changes in Ted.

Despite his death and resurrection, Ted feels better than ever before. The novel observes that Street—even without a regularly functioning body—seemed more alive than ever: "He [Street] felt oddly alive, though he couldn't feel his heart thumping in his chest" (22).[3] Even his sex life with his wife, Gloria, improves after his body's "death." In a rather absurd sex scene, Ted's wife touches the stitches that held on his severed head until she "moaned and moaned and bucked and bucked and had what must have been a dozen orgasms" (49). At least as described by Everett, once Ted's mind is free from his body, he can satisfy his wife in a way that was impossible before his "accident," or perhaps Gloria feels free to satisfy her own desires once Street's head is disconnected from his body. In any case, as a result of Ted's death and resurrection, Gloria becomes more attuned to her own body. Ted soon discovers that it is not merely his sexual desire that becomes intensified but all of his sensory experiences become heightened: "As all of his senses were so acutely awake to the world, the absence of any stimuli emanating from himself became notable. There was no heartbeat of course but neither was there a gurgling in his stomach or a rumbling from any region below" (23). Everett, here and throughout the novel, depicts the body as a mental distraction that limits Street from realizing his intellectual and moral potential. The narrative notes that it is only after Ted Street's mind has been severed from its body that he can actually cry and release his anger, frustration, and self-doubt (29). His newfound ability to express his emotions allows him to be more sensitive to the needs of his wife and children. This includes protecting them from the media frenzy that stems from his resurrection.

Ted's resurrection has provided him with a certain mental clarity that he lacked before his death. He begins truly to understand how important his wife and children are to him. Because of his death and then rebirth, Street becomes a media sensation and cameramen camp outside his house with the hopes of getting an interview. One reporter, Barbie Becker, makes a false report that Ted's daughter, Emily, is the victim of some form of child abuse (74–75). While the old Ted Street would have lacked the ability to negotiate this terrain, this new "heady," more astute and aware version can sense the real Barbie Becker beneath her media façade, and he uses that knowledge to free his daughter from Child Protective Services (78). He also grants Becker's request for an interview. However, when the reporter fails to bring Emily with her to the interview, Street demands, on live television, the return of his daughter before continuing with the interview. He threatens to humiliate Becker with embarrassing information he has learned about her if she does not live up to her end of the bargain (80–81). Once the reporter engineers the return of his daughter, Ted agrees to the interview. Moments before the interview, Becker's hand touches Street's and he learns that he has the ability to see her past merely through physical contact (84). With this knowledge, Street responds to the reporter's questions with his own questions about her life and the choices she has made. This derails and confuses Becker, causing her to cry and claim that he is mean. Street replies: "No, Ms. Becker, I used to be . . . I used to be just like you and I guess that's how it is that I see so much of you. I didn't intend to be cruel, only truthful. This truth thing is new to me" (86). While television news seeks to create a packaged version of reality, Ted's mind—when freed from his bodily concerns—gains the ability to see through the media spectacle, including the very role they want him to play in their mediated version of his story. But the media are not the only ones interested in Ted.

Amid anonymous phone calls telling him he is the devil, Dr. Timmons, a specialist in cryogenics from the USC Medical School, contacts Ted Street because she wants to examine him (55–56). In this section of the novel, Everett parodies science's attempt to understand life and death, as he implicitly compares Dr. Timmons, the research scientist, with Dr. Dume, a medical expert regularly featured on the news. Dr. Dume announces that "for the medical profession, death is not a precise moment or instant, but a continuous process" (57). After some comical question by another news anchor about decapitation and death throes, Dr. Dume concludes: "All these questions. I think it's obvious that this is a hoax. Maybe, he was never dead" (58). However, when Dr. Timmons actually examines Street, she concludes that he lacks a pulse and thus is dead, despite his apparent brain activity. She ultimately tells a reporter that "The man [Street] is dead, yet he is still alive. His heart is not beating, but his brain continues to function. I don't understand it. I don't have any answers for you. He's frightened, I think. I too am frightened . . . Maybe we should all be frightened" (68). Neither Dr. Dume nor Dr. Timmons can provide answers to these life-and-death questions about the relationship between the mind and the body. By painting a scientist and a medical doctor as equally befuddled, Everett criticizes science for its supposed monopoly on knowledge and truth and the media for creating the illusion that scientists possess answers to philosophical questions. It is this impasse between scientific and media knowledge that concludes the first section of the novel, revealing the epistemological limit of these ways of knowing.

Book Two begins with Ted admitting to Gloria that he had his accident while driving to commit suicide (92–93). After this admission, Ted realizes that he cannot hide in his house and decides again to try to live a normal life. So, he plugs his phone back into the wall: "he refuse[s] to be held prisoner" in his house and decides that his family should go shopping (96). When the Streets open their garage, get into their van, and drive away, the reporters are so shocked and unprepared that the family is able to escape to the grocery store without any problems. However, once they arrive there, other customers notice them and soon the news reporters make their arrival. As the chaos begins to descend on the store, Ted suggests that the family ought "to slip out the back" (98). However, as they make their escape, Ted is kidnapped—thrown into a sack and then carried by several men to a van (99). When Ted tries to speak, one of the men tells him: "Shut up, you devil" (100)—repeating the language of an earlier crank call Street received (52).[4] At this point, it is unclear exactly who has abducted Street, but the repetition of the devil taunt foreshadows this section's satiric representation of religion. Much like his earlier depictions of science and the media, Everett's choice to introduce religion through these taunts and insults illustrates his critical view of American religion. Rather than depicting Christianity as providing metaphysical guidance and morality, the novel portrays religion as hateful, fearful, and the exact opposite of what it purports to offer humankind. Given that the name Ted or Theodore means "gift of god" in Greek, Everett is clearly having a bit of fun where Big Daddy, the leader of a religious cult, and his followers mistake this divine gift for the devil.

During his abduction, Street learns Big Daddy is the leader of the cult. Here, Everett is obviously playing with Christian depictions of God as a heavenly father. Indeed, Big Daddy is a fat white man with a large beard and white hair, vaguely reminiscent of Santa Claus (105).[5] His followers are clearly terrified of Street, and Big Daddy speaks in a parody of King James English as he leads them in this battle against Ted Street, their ideal-ized vision of one of Satan's spawns. When Street asks to use a bathroom, Big Daddy tells a follower: "Take this demon to the toilet and stay with him . . . but do not look at his organ nor his excretions directly. Observe them, if you must, through the safety of the mirror" (107). In both his de-piction of Big Daddy and the religious leader's response to Street, Everett accentuates the role of physical bodies in his account (see also 130–31). For example, Big Daddy supports his connection to the divine with the absurd fact that "God blessed me [Big Daddy] with good-smelling feet" (108).[6] Through these examples, Everett illustrates the many anxieties Big Daddy possesses regarding his body and how these anxieties became central com-ponents of his religious vision.

The group's fear of Street is particularly focused on his body and the temptations of the flesh, implicitly positing a necessary connection be-tween this putative devil's body and his ultimate goals. Despite being kid-napped by this strange band of religious folk, however, "the more they tried to bully him, the calmer he [Street] felt and he remembered the ad-vice he'd always heard about surviving quicksand, relax and swim out" (102). Street's "calm" reveals itself through his mockery of the group's fear of his body. He jokingly mentions to Gerald, one of Big Daddy's follow-ers, that "devils are actually very clean . . . you'd be surprised how fas-tidious Satan himself is. He won't talk to anybody until he's washed his face in the morning" (108). In these sections and others, Everett re-frames the battle—no matter how comic or ridiculous—into a contest over the meaning and care of the body. Partially mocking the history of Christianity in which witchcraft or evil was read through the body, Everett asserts the importance of the body as key signifier for determining morality and spirituality.

As the novel proceeds, Street learns more about Big Daddy and his religious beliefs, including his belief in aliens, the coming conflagration, and his sexual exploitation of the women in his group under the guise of religious indoctrination. Big Daddy claims to have seen "six angelic beings" (121) and teaches that "Angels don't have wings . . . what people think are wings is really only the light from the spaceship. The ship travels by the refraction of light" and is the "chariot of Gods" (123). Big Daddy and his followers are preparing for a "war that's coming, the war against evil, against you [Street, who represents the devil], against the government, against the black helicopters" (125). The group has been stockpiling weapons for this battle. Big Daddy, however, has a preference for older weapons that cause slower, potentially more gruesome deaths, because "slow [killing] is better, gives the heathens a chance to find the LordJesusGodalmighty and repent" (127). Because he prophesizes about the coming war, Big Daddy also feels the need to "comfort his sheep." This comfort is primarily sexual and Big Daddy "initiate[s] them [his female followers] into the world of complete surrender to the Godeverelasting." He frames this as his own service to God, which in turn results in the production of babies and the future generation (132). Street later learns that Big Daddy has kidnapped many children and keeps them in a bunker to use as a bargaining chip if the authorities ever wish to arrest him (147).

The group's religion, despite its spiritual aspirations, remains remarkably tethered to the body, its pleasures, and its suffering.[7] By focusing on Ted Street, the mind without a pulsing body, Big Daddy, in effect, is declaring war on the mind. However, Big Daddy focuses his punishment on Street's body. Illustrative of this, Big Daddy announces that "we've decided to torture you [Street] for a while . . . I've always wanted to torture the anti-Christ, to lacerate a reaching limb of the devil himself" (133). He also tells his followers his ultimate intention to destroy Street: "The devil's ass is mine. We'll keep him for a couple of days and then we'll shoot him with a cannon, blow him to smithereens" (134). After some elaborate planning for Ted's execution, Big Daddy decides to eradicate Ted and the devil. However, things don't go quite as planned. The cannonball "did not miss his [Ted's] body but neither did it pass through him. It hit his chest with a perceptible thump and fell to the ground at Ted's feet. Ted had never heard a hush as silent and heavy as the one that fell over that dusty yard" (145). Once he fails to demolish the demon's body, Big Daddy is "shaken" and his followers begin to disperse (146). Ted is forgotten and ultimately is able to escape. Big Daddy's failure to control the devil's body, thus, culminates Book Two. Religion, or at least Big Daddy's version of it, is no more successful than either science or the media in understanding the mind-body split. Moreover, Big Daddy's cult reads Street's resurrection not as confirmation of Christianity or a connection to Jesus, but as a challenge designed by the devil to ensnare the innocent. This allows Everett to continue his ongoing critique of Christianity.

Like Moses in the Bible, Book Three opens with Ted Street wandering in the desert. Unlike the ancient Israelites, however, Street does not find the Promised Land. Rather, the government swoops down and captures him, hoping to transform his powers into a new military weapon. They take Street to a secret research facility in Roswell, New Mexico. In a second narrative thread in this section, Gloria Street tries to collect the proceeds of Ted's life insurance policy. This results in a pretty funny conversation in which the agent states that he has seen Ted Street alive on television. Gloria then replies, "actually, I have a death certificate from the medical examiner's office" (155). The reader ultimately learns that Gloria is making her claim in order to get the insurance company to hire a detective and find her kidnapped husband. What these two plotlines share is how the very functioning of government and business is linked to knowledge about the body. On the one hand, both government and corporations seek to abstract identity from the body as part of its reliance on modernist strategies for understanding, classifying, and deploying knowledge. On the other hand, these entities continually need to reintegrate these abstract or mental conceptions with the body to ground their claims to knowledge. In this comic section, Everett narrates the hopes for and frequent failure to reintegrate the discursive and the physical realms.

As Ted Street is toured around the underground government facility, he wonders if he will find Lucius Brockway, the infamous character from *Invisible Man* who created optic white paint and who, in his paranoia, almost kills the novel's eponymous hero (163). While Street is being led around by Clancy, who is not clearly raced but is probably white, Everett notes for the reader that Ted encounters "an incredibly handsome young lieutenant ... with deep-set brown eyes, his skin an even mahogany," named Dudley (164). Ultimately, his tour culminates in the "Re-Animation Death and Intravital Carpophoric Anaplastics Laboratory," abbreviated as "RADICAL" (165). When Street first observes the lab's director, he is confused by the deep voice of the female Dr. Lyons (165). Before he even gets to describe the strange experiments in the lab, Everett sets the stage by invoking a series of raced and gendered bodies (from Brockway to Dudley to Dr. Lyons) that frustrate the observer's gaze. Of Dr. Lyons, Everett writes that "Ted knew by the way Dr. Lyons carried herself toward him from her desk, from the sound of her heart beating within her chest, that she was not a she at all, but a man" (165). A few sentences later, the novel states that "in spite of the fact that she possessed, or at one time did possess, a penis and testicles, the doctor cut a fine example of a woman" (165). These references work to highlight the failure of modernity to reintegrate mind and body, despite the promise of modern scientific discourse to solve all sorts of contemporary challenges.

In the first few moments of their conversation, Dr. Lyons begins to reveal to Street the nature of her work: "What you probably don't know is that people have been coming back to life, so to speak, for as long as humans have walked the face of the planet" (166). Her research is focused on understanding this conundrum. Then, Lyons tells Street why she is interested in him particularly: "I'm going to find out why you did [survive decapitation] even if it kills you" (167). At this point, Clancy reenters the room and explains to Ted why the government is funding this research: "Because you are apparently a man who can't be killed . . . Imagine an army of men like you" (167). After running a series of tests, Dr. Lyons pronounces that Ted is "a perfectly healthy dead man" (180). Then, she tells him that she will do an autopsy of sorts on him, but assures him that Street will feel no pain because his body is functionally dead. After cutting him open and removing organs, Ted asks if Dr. Lyons will "be putting every-thing back." She replies "if you like . . . but you don't seem to need it" (182). At the conclusion of the autopsy, Ted queries Dr. Lyons whether she has learned anything. She does not respond, but Everett describes that "her demeanor had changed. The tough pretense was gone and all that remained was fear" (183). Obviously, this scene is quite humorous, mock-ing how scientific inquiry operates. But, more significantly, it suggests that examinations of merely physical or material reality cannot explain what it means to be alive. Such narrow inquiries fail to capture the very real way that mind and body work together to create consciousness and the experi-ence of being human.

After being cut open and having his organs removed and then rein-serted, Street decides to try to escape from this facility. He announces to his guards that he will be leaving and they shoot him. Of course, this does not work because he is already dead: "Ted was amazed but not surprised by the missing effect of the bullets. Clearly, he could not be killed. Whether a function of the fact that he was already dead he could not say. Ironically, he thought, if the young men had tackled and subdued him he would have been unable to break free. Their bullets having passed harmlessly through their mark, the soldiers fainted" (191). Successfully negotiating the chal-lenge the guards presented, Street commences his escape.

Wandering through the research facility, he encounters Oswald Avery, a scientist who lost his funding and is waiting to learn his fate—not un-like how Street's tenure denial precipitated his "death" (194–95). Avery then proceeds to show Street around his reanimation lab, and Street sees "twenty dark-haired drooling men dressed in jumpsuits." Some were "bad-ly deformed," others were "hunchbacked," and "one man had three legs" (196–97). Avery then explains that these bodies were his failed attempts to clone Jesus as he is "the most famous reanimated person" (197). He then reveals that the cloned Jesuses possess brains as broken as their bodies and that he has already killed a number of the failed versions (198). Avery asks Street if he believes Jesus was the son of God. Street admits that he does not and then Avery claims that he has to believe as his "funding depends on it" (198). Street's discovery of Avery's research begins to tie together the novel's many strands, connecting the mind-body problem with sci-ence and religion. For Everett, Jesus is a particular problem for religion and science because he exemplifies how the mind and body cannot be easily linked. Neither discourse provides a ready answer for the life and death of Jesus. Within the binary logic offered by the mind-body split, the very research facility itself, with its underground bunkers, its labyrinthine hallways, and its high-tech equipment, seems to represent a mind or brain that is completely disconnected from material reality. One could argue that the failure of Avery's experiments result from science's inability to integrate the mental and the physical. Or from another angle of vision, Avery's research is seeking to turn the bodies of the reanimated Jesus into a mere military instrument, thereby severing the body of Jesus from his/God's intelligence.

With his funding failing and little future of being allowed to leave the secret military facility due to the sensitive nature of his research, Avery agrees to help Street escape. For Avery, the choices are either death within the research facility or be killed trying to escape. Avery describes this situation as being "afraid to live" (205). While Avery prepares himself to leave the facility, Street notices that "Jesus 19" seems to have a functioning mind. Although he did lack a mouth (and thus cannot speak), Jesus 19 demonstrates his "divinity" by merely responding to Street's gaze, not in horror or sympathy, but in a human way (207). Jesus 19's potential divinity despite his bodily "defect" highlights the central tension in the novel regarding the mind-body split. Through the misreading of Jesus 19's body, Avery and science fail to grasp the true nature of his being and his mind. Once he is ready, Avery reveals that the "cadaver disposal chute" (213) is their most likely route to safety and freedom as that is ground level.

When they exit from the cadaver disposal system, Avery, Jesus 19, and Street find themselves nearly blinded by sunlight, an allusion to Plato's "Allegory of the Cave" (223). Quickly, they find a hut in which to hide until dark. Then, they steal a Hummer truck and drive it through multiple fences until they have escaped the military facility. Waiting outside are hundreds of civilians who camp outside the Roswell facility, thinking it contains aliens and possesses some kind of mystical power (228–29). The trio (or trinity) is welcomed by the crowd, especially as they recognize Ted Street (from all the publicity surrounding his reanimation) and identify him as the "true Messiah" (230). The Heavenly Order of Pyromantic of the *Ruach Elohim* hides the trio[8] in their campers and treats them as saviors.

Everett cannot help himself from commenting on the absurdity of his own fictional creation: "Ted had been elevated from devil to messiah. The irony was too great for Avery to contain his laughter as the three of them stood alone" (231). Through the character of Avery, Everett notes further: "Imagine that . . . calling you [Street] the Messiah right in front of old Jesus Christ here" (231). Now that they have been saved from the military complex, the Heavenly Order of Pyromantic of the *Ruach Elohim* prepares a ceremony to honor Ted Street, their putative messiah. However, Street escapes their clutches so that he can alert the authorities to the children locked in Big Daddy's camp and so that he can return home (239–41). This ends Book Three. In this section of *American Desert* Everett reveals the failure of contemporary religion and science to link the mind and the body. For Everett, modern philosophical notions about the mind/body split have created the impasse between faith and reason and caused science and religion to become deformed caricatures of themselves.

Ultimately, Ted saves the children and returns home, as outlined in Book Four. However, Street finds that he cannot simply fall back into his previous habits or routine, now that he has experienced this existential crisis. The novel ends with Street inviting Barbie Becker back into his home for a final interview, which is really just a monologue. In this final statement, Street tries to explain what he has learned about life and death.

> I am dead. I died and I am dead and I can tell you no more about the meaning of life than I could when I was alive. But I know everything about the meaning of death. I saw no white light, attractive or otherwise. I felt no sweet feeling of relief or understanding or ease. I felt nothing. Happily, I can also report that I experienced no pain. However, now I am nothing but pain. To myself, my family, and to you. (290)

Street also asserts the he is no messiah and no savior. He also tries to tell his audience that they ought not to fear death. With that, he looks at his family and then removes the stitches that connected his head to his body. Then, "Ted grabbed his head between his two hands, removed it and set it in his lap, closed his eyes, and stayed dead" (291). And thus ends the novel. While most comic novels seek to reintegrate its warring parts, *American Desert* culminates by highlighting Ted Street's failure to heal the breach between his mind and his dead body. Once he realizes that the synthesis is impossible, he, in effect, completes the suicide he contemplated in the novel's opening.[9]

Clearly, *American Desert* engages in a "thought" experiment about the relationship of mind and body, the meaning of life and death, and how science and religion try to provide answers to these questions. While there are a handful of references to race, the novel is not a particularly raced one, nor does it explicitly engage the tradition of the African American novel. Moreover, Everett's resistance to being identified as an "African American writer" might enable readers to simply avoid questions of race altogether. By cataloging the many ways that minds and bodies are mutually dependent, the novel, however, implicitly frustrates efforts to engage in a color-blind reading of this work and Everett's work more generally. Seemingly contradicting his own reading of his oeuvre, Everett in *American Desert* asserts again and again that the mind and body are linked in essential ways. The meaning of life cannot be viewed in either physical or mental/spiritual terms alone. The very critique that Everett mobilizes against religion and science underlines that their relative failures result from their inability to fully integrate the mind and the body or the spiritual and the physical.

In the introduction, I observed that *American Desert* should be read as a "postmodern allegory about the perils of abstract identities." Much of the comedy of the novel follows from this abstraction of specific bodies into symbols, whether it is the transformation of Street into a devil/messiah, Barbie Becker into a media star, or Big Daddy into a religious leader. These characters seem relatively thin or perhaps they seem like mere caricatures. Yet, *American Desert*, despite its comedy and irony, has a serious message about allowing individuals to flourish in their full complexity. For Everett, the goal of reintegrating minds and bodies—our mental musings and our physical experiences—has become more challenging as knowledge has increasingly become separated into discrete disciplines or categories. As a result, Everett depicts science, religion, the government, and the media as presenting partial views, which have become increasingly fundamentalist as they create their own bunkers; hence, the isolated camps of Big Daddy and the military scientists, and self-perpetuating media spectacles. Street's existential crisis, resulting from his decapitation and reanimation, illustrates the need to bring these isolated individuals together into a more coherent whole. Everett's call for reintegration, however, is decidedly post-modern in that as much as he asserts the need for this kind of wholeness he seems to doubt that any transcendence is possible. As a result, a reani-mated Ted Street cannot heal the breach caused by the mind-body split and he must die.

While there has been relatively little scholarly discussion of the novel thus far, *American Desert* is a significant work in Everett's corpus and speaks to ongoing concerns about contemporary African American literary pro-duction. In 1988, Trey Ellis's "New Black Aesthetic" rejected earlier theories based on essentialist foundations that suggested one's body determined, or should determine, the consciousness of one's mind and one's art. Ev-erett certainly shares Ellis's concerns. Writers such as Colson Whitehead, Michael Thomas, and Martha Southgate, among other contemporary Af-rican American writers, are struggling to figure out how to represent Afri-can Americans in literature without succumbing to essentialist rhetoric. Scholars, as exemplified by the *African American Review*'s 2007 special issue related to post-soul aesthetics, are similarly engaged in creating critical vocabulary to analyze and understand these new forms of racial represen-tation. *American Desert* complicates any effort to frame Everett as a writer who is post-race or views race as a mere cultural construct or as something to transcend. My reading of *American Desert* highlights that race matters not because it is an essence that determines a person's thoughts and ex-periences but because material conditions affect and shape a person's consciousness. While Everett frequently appears as cynic, *American Desert* reveals his hope that perhaps one day African American writers can rein-tegrate their minds with their bodies without succumbing to racial deter-minism or essentialism.

Notes

1. The editors of this volume have brilliantly pointed out that one could read the phrase "Ted's death, departure, demise, dissolution" to foreshadow the novel's four main parts.

2. Ted Street's father suffered from Alzheimer's disease, providing another instance when bodies and minds get severed (60–61). See also *Erasure* in which Monk's mother loses much of her mind as a result of Alzheimer's.

3. In the pages that follow, the narrator notes that "He felt strangely that without the sound of his heart, his ears were even more open to the sounds around him . . . He was able to smell the spearmint of the driver's gum . . . As all of his senses were acutely awake to the world" (23).

4. Big Daddy's labeling of Street as the devil and his later admonishment about looking directly at his penis may hint that Street is, in fact, black. While there is not sufficient evidence to prove or disprove the case, both comments might make more sense in this racial context.

5. Later, Big Daddy is described as wearing red clothes (133).

6. Through his new ability to see an individual's past by touching them, Street learns that Big Daddy's father beat him, berated him, and accused him of being filthy (109–10). This explanation for Big Daddy's beliefs further cements the link between bodies and divinity within American culture.

7. In an ironic repetition of the Hebrew Bible, Big Daddy's compound resides in the desert, hence the book's title, *American Desert*. While Moses communicated with God in the Sinai Desert, Big Daddy's sojourn in the desert is depicted as false prophesy. According to Everett, the desert is the site for religious experience precisely because it is a place of physical extremes, which affects both the body and the mind. Through his use of the desert as the home of crazy religious groups and, in Book Three, bizarre government agencies, Everett shows how the religious experiences within the Bible require a mind-body link.

8. This trio of Avery, Jesus 19, and Street could also be read as a parodic version of the trinity as Avery is the "father" of Jesus 19 and Street certainly could be viewed as a ghost, given his reanimation.

9. Beatty, in his equally satirical novel *White Boy Shuffle*, posits suicide as a "solution" to the problems faced by contemporary African Americans.

Chapter 6

A Bird of a Different Feather

Blues, Jazz, and the Difficult Journey to the Self in Percival Everett's Suder

UZZIE CANNON

Much of the recent critical interest in Percival Everett's literary contribution focuses on the author's seemingly easy ability to move beyond race in his novels. Indeed, Everett indirectly resists being identified as any specific type of writer, even an African American writer, as he explains, "I don't want to talk about race . . . I just want to make art."[1] Of course, his aesthetic observations are not without precedent. Black American writers as diverse as Charles Chesnutt, Jean Toomer, Zora Neale Hurston, Anne Petry, Richard Wright, and James Baldwin have all written fiction that purports to be "raceless."[2] But like them, this is not to say that Everett's fiction avoids race; rather, often in his work, race within a *specifically* African American cultural experience is not always foregrounded. Instead, when characters in Everett's novels happen to be racially identified as African American, one could argue that they perform a "postmodern" blackness in which their experiences as *human beings* transcend race.

Significant to Everett's theorization of race in his fiction is satire and parody, and he has made it clear that in addition to African American writers and thinkers, his work has been influenced by the likes of Euro-American literary and popular cultural figures as eclectic as Laurence Stern, Samuel Butler, Mark Twain, Groucho Marx, and Bullwinkle.[3] Further, while satire and parody tend to pervade his oeuvre, the author appropriates in typical postmodern fashion other narrative strategies to tell a story. Everett experiments with absurd characterization, unpredictable plots, and nonlinear time that in some ways have marginalized him as an

African/American writer. Certainly, for Everett, this is not necessarily a bad thing, for his position as an "experimental" African/American writer reflects what LeRoi Jones/Amiri Baraka wrote almost fifty years ago about the then-contemporary African American literary scene: "There are now a great many young black writers in America who do realize that their customary isolation from the mainstream is a valuable way into any description they might make of an America. . . . The vantage point is classically perfect—outside and inside at the same time" (*Home: Social Essays* 164). One can certainly see how Everett, as a writer, works outside and inside of African American and Euro-American literary traditions. In many of his fictions, the characters are not racially marked as black or white. And this, as Everett is well aware of, may or may not affect the way one reads these stories. Yet, despite his resistance to his work being seen as always already race-specific, Everett's first novel, *Suder* (1983), continues in, yet significantly diverges from, the African American literary tradition. While *Suder* eschews the "social realism" and "dialect tradition"⁴ that some critics seem to suggest ultimately defines the African American literary tradition, the novel represents through its protagonist, Craig Suder, a text significant to the study of contemporary "postmodern" African American literary representation.

Often comic, the novel portrays through flashbacks of his childhood Craig Suder's struggle with his inability to value himself on his own terms; it is an existential crisis that frames most postmodern narratives written by both black and white writers. Moreover, the nonlinear plot showcases unpredictability and absurdity that is also a hallmark of postmodern literature. Everett's postmodern fiction, in the words of Bernard Bell, "moves beyond modernism of the 1950s in an effort to expand the possibilities of the novel and to reconstruct the liberated lives of the generation of the 1960s" (283). The deployment of postmodern narrative strategies by post-1970s black writers allowed them to begin to more radically redefine "blackness" in all its variances. Certainly, Everett's portrayal of Craig Suder's journey toward self-mastery is an important trope in the African American literary tradition with Margaret Russett having claimed that *Suder* is "[p]robably the 'blackest' of all" Everett's novels (360). Yet, however sincere Russett's statement might be, her proclamation risks espousing an essentialized notion of blackness, something falling into the trap of essentializing that many of Everett's narratives work to circumvent. Yet, as my analysis of *Suder* will demonstrate, even if "race" in its most political form is not at the heart of the novel, Craig Suder's journey to selfhood is indicative of what it means to be a black man in contemporary America. This essay argues that Everett's use of a nonlinear plot, coupled with a blues and jazz aesthetic, produces a site in *Suder* for revisioning the representation of black masculinity.

Psychologists Joseph L. White and James H. Cones III contend that in order for more diverse views of black masculinity to evolve in American society black men will need to establish themselves outside the confines of an established patriarchal paradigm: a mindset that says real men are white, heterosexual, and individualists guided by philosophies that rest upon dualist ways of negotiating the world. In order to break free of this paradigm, White and Cones insist that black men must turn to "improvisation, resilience, connectedness to others, the value of direct experience, and spirituality" (48). These strategies for freedom and self-mastery underpin much of African American aesthetic production, as black writers often draw from blues and jazz musical traditions that suggest alternative ways of understanding and ordering the world" (10). Everett's consideration of the liberatory potential of blues and jazz in *Suder* is framed by jazz saxophonist Charlie "Bird" Parker's much-heralded 1946 recording of "Ornithology." Working within a blues and jazz musical tradition, Everett specifically draws on testifying and improvisation, standard features of blues and jazz music, to unfetter Suder from family and career expectations that impede his self-mastery.[5] However, whereas blues and jazz as a trope in African American literature traditionally has been used to symbolize transcendence, technically and thematically in *Suder*, a postmodern novel, blues and jazz work as a vehicle to convey what French philosopher Gilles Deleuze calls immanence in the production of subject formation and self-actualization. Deleuze theorizes that "the synthesis of consciousness" is passive and based on a series of related, habitual experiences that, over time, are constantly updated (Smith and Protevi n.p.). In other words, for Deleuze, subject formation, similar to the blues and particularly jazz aesthetics, is underpinned by improvisation. Indeed, W. Lawrence Hogue observes, "We are beginning to discern and appreciate how the blues [and by extension jazz] definition of life is just another representation of the

African American" (170). Indeed, as Everett makes clear in *Suder*, jazz and the blues mark singular, not monolithic, ways of representing African American life via artistic production.

Blues music generally began among black rural populations as an oral and vernacular-based musical form that welcomed a variety of inflections, sometimes joyful, sometimes melancholy for those participating in its production. While there resides an overarching structure underlying the music, blues narratives "suggest change, movement, action, continuance, unlimited and unending possibility" (Baker 8). Moreover, as Albert Murray has written, the blues "affirms that which is upstanding in human nature, that which stands out against the overwhelming odds of the non-human and anti-human elements of the universe" (43).

In this regard, Baker and Murray position the blues as a strategy for survival as potentially but not necessarily transcendent. Nevertheless, Hogue asserts, "It [the blues] functions counter-hegemonically within society, defining the African American (male) outside features, characteristics and definitions of the white/black binary that dominates the social reality in the United States" (147). It would appear that a blues aesthetic would seem to fit perfectly with Everett's insistence on breaking down binary conceptualizations that promote epistemological and ontological stasis and hinder individual freedom; however, my analysis of Craig Suder's childhood and adolescence will show how, ultimately, Everett rejects a blues aesthetic as unsatisfactory for the kind of liberation and self-affirmation that drives Suder in his adulthood. Instead, I will argue that as an adult Suder adopts a jazz-inflected way of living in the restrictive world that motivates his unorthodox journey in search of his "true" self.

According to blues theorists, call-and-response, testifying, blues notes, and the "standard" twelve-bar songs can be telltale signs of blues in narrative. These blues qualities can manifest structurally and thematically in literary narratives often through speech, characterization, and setting. "Testifying," or bearing witness to one's trials and (potentially) overcoming them, appears to be the method of blues expression in certain novels where the narrative perspective is first-person and the protagonist encounters conflict within the plot. The blues persona relates his or her experience by testifying in a manner as exemplified in the following standard twelve-bar AAB lines from bluesman Keb' Mo':

I ain't got no woman but I don't feel sad
I ain't got no woman but I don't feel sad
Cause the woman that was with me treated
me so dirty, low-down, and bad. (Polygram 2000)

Keb' Mo's "Dirty, Low Down and Bad" demonstrates how "[t]he persona of the individual performer entirely dominates the song which centers upon the singer's own feelings, experiences, . . . , acquaintances, idiosyncrasies" (Levine 222). In relating his or her troubles, the blues person testifies in the *hope* of overcoming them. In expressing Suder's blues as a child, Everett delivers the blues aesthetic in a thematic and structured manner, as he uses testimonial dialogue to express the character's discontentment, as a young man, with his home life, and initially, as an adult, with his family and his failing baseball career.

While Everett does not specifically pattern *Suder* on traditional blues or jazz aesthetic formulations, a kind of "postmodern" blues aesthetic pervades the flashback, childhood, chapters of the novel, while a "postmodern" jazz aesthetic is evidenced in the scenes that relate to Suder's adulthood. Craig Suder relates his life story through a narrative back-and-forth that works as improvisation, as the reader learns of his need to escape various personal and career pressures that weigh upon him. The blues motif works particularly well for articulating young Suder's problems at home. Stephen Henderson's assertion that the blues "are a music and a *poetry* of confrontation—with the self, with the family and loved ones, with the oppressive forces of society, with nature, and, on the heaviest level, with fate and the universe itself" (qtd. in Nicholes 93, original emphasis), illustrates young Suder's life. Suder's adult life, however, evolves and is "acted out in jazz moments" that allow him to "view his life through the prism of an improvised musical solo" (Hawkins xxi). His journey to selfhood, as an adult, possesses a cosmopolitan edge that allows for interaction with the world outside the home. From this improvisation emerges an African American psychology that demonstrates Suder's refiguration of the self.

As a young boy, however, Craig Suder experiences a "blues-inflected" childhood. His home life is quite dysfunctional, as we learn of his mother's mental illness and his often sad but comic struggle to deal with it, his father's general indifference toward her suffering, and his brother Martin's burgeoning sociopathic behavior. Young Suder's blues-state evinces moments in which he tries to develop a way of engaging in the world that is radically different from other members of his family. We are immediately privy to the source of Suder's childhood blues when his father first informs him of his mother's "craziness." In a heartbreakingly comic moment, the family members gather around the kitchen table and Suder's father bluntly states, "Boys, your mother is crazy" (7). Without hesitation, the mother agrees; and with little concern with Craig's or his brother's reaction to this bombshell, she abruptly leaves the kitchen to work in the garden. In utter confusion, Suder starts crying. This incident marks the beginning of his existential crisis. I would argue, however, that this scene is counter to a "typical blues" expressive moment that might point to a way for Suder "to keep the painful details and episodes of a brutal experience alive in one's aching consciousness, to finger the jagged grain, and to transcend it, not by the consolation of philosophy but by squeezing from it a near-tragic, near-comic lyricism" (Ellison, qtd. in Baker 133). In other words, Suder does not laugh to keep from crying. As a young man, he is not yet able to develop coping mechanisms, a mask of joy, behind which to hide his pain.

In a number of comic moments, Suder's blues become apparent. For instance, when Kathy, Suder's mother, brags to him, "You're like me. You're just like your mother, just like your mother" (*Suder* 14), she exacerbates his fears and frustrations because he is convinced that he will inherit his mother's insanity. He continues to bear the brunt of her illness as she comically subjects him to waterless baths and conspiratorial plots to catch his father committing adultery with Lou Ann Narramore, who works at the local pharmacy. In addition, his mother is obsessed with her concern that Suder has been "pulling on himself" (60), which keeps him despondent and impotent in trying to convince her otherwise.

In another incident that fuels his childhood blues, Suder's mother decides to race around the entire town of Fayetteville, North Carolina, for no apparent reason. In order to practice the finish of her marathon, she snatches the tissue out of the family bathroom, drapes it across "one oak tree to another on one side of the yard" (126), and breaks through it in order to demonstrate her imagined heroic finish—all while an embarrassed and confused Suder sits on the toilet, paperless. When he confronts her about her embarrassing antics, she slaps him, leaving him further frustrated and confused (126).

Despite his blues, however, Suder tries to respond to his mother's instability with compassion. He does not distance himself from her as his brother, Martin, does. Instead, he tries to change his mother's behavior; he does not passively stand by as she spirals out of control. Fed up with her bizarre behavior, he decides to "hit her on the head and knock some sense into her" (8), after Martin randomly broaches the idea. When this has no effect, except to render her unconscious, his anxiety and fear increases; yet, he seemingly remains optimistic. He attempts to palliate his mother's outlandish behavior by choosing to focus on those moments when she seems lucid, even when Martin reminds him that "Asking everybody [at church] to move out of the first three rows was pretty crazy" (13). When Martin tells Suder, "She really oughta be put someplace," he defensively exclaims, "She's our mother" (74). He further demonstrates his love and compassion for his mother when she makes a valiant effort to complete the marathon, but in the final stages of the race, she wants to give up. Suder quickly runs out to her, along with his father, to provide encouragement. Their support spurs her on to finish the race and she falls to her knees crying in triumph. At this point, Suder, although not completely certain, begins to see his mother as *perhaps* not crazy but simply eccentric.

One of the more telling aspects about Suder's childhood blues is that we never really witness his father's active involvement in helping him through his difficulties. During this impressionable time, Suder does not receive guidance or support from his father about "how to be a man." His father, as breadwinner, appears unresponsive to his emotional needs surrounding the onset of puberty and his mother's mental illness. Most of the conversations that take place between them include disparaging remarks about the mother, which does nothing to assuage his blues. Moreover, his older brother hinders his healthy psychological development because he also does little to provide brotherly guidance and advice to help Suder overcome his melancholy. Suder lives with the blues because he has no viable (black) male support system to help mitigate his frustrations. And while he is able to offer his mother much-needed succor, in short, a blues-inflected ontology does not provide him even the possibility of emotional and psychological relief. His blues remain unalleviated.

Nevertheless, as the story progresses, Suder's compassion toward his mother deepens when he encounters Bud Powell, a jazz musician, who subsequently bequeaths him the nickname "Bird." In real life, Bud Powell was a friend of Charlie "Bird" Parker and a fellow bebop jazz musician. He often jammed with Parker and challenged him to be more innovative in the development of his craft. In the novel, the fictional Bud Powell challenges Suder's view that his mother's bizarre behavior necessarily means that she is crazy. One day while Bud is playing his rendition of Parker's "Ornithology," Suder walks in to listen. Upon hearing the song, he comments, "That's pretty . . . . That's real pretty" (76). As the two continue to converse, Suder learns that the song is considered "jazz" and that, according to Powell, "Jazz is life" (76). Through his appreciation of "Ornithology," the freedom and flight imagined in Parker's song become, for Suder, synonymous with life. Moreover, Powell's friendship and mentoring helps him see his mother as "[m]aybe not crazy. . . . Maybe just different" (77), which helps to free her from his often harsh criticism. Suder's encounter with "Ornithology" begins his transformation from blues-child to jazz free-bird.

In the novel, Everett associates Suder's jazz transformation with nature—birds in particular. While Everett does not pattern Suder on traditional blues or jazz formulations, a kind of postmodern blues aesthetic pervades the flashback chapters of the novel, and a postmodern jazz aesthetics is evidenced in the scenes that take place in the novel's present, Suder's adulthood. Craig Suder narrates his life story through a back-and-forth intermingling of childhood and adulthood moments that narratively resemble jazz improvisation. Through Everett's jazz-inspired technique, the reader learns of Suder's deep desire to escape the many pressures he encounters throughout his boyhood due to his dysfunctional family situation. Moreover, Everett demonstrates how the blues carry over into Suder's adult life as he attempts to deal with dysfunction in his own family as well as his failing baseball career. The blues motif works particularly well for articulating the young Suder's problems at home, since the blues stems more directly from personal matters about home and hearth. As an adult, his journey of self-discovery is best rendered through a jazz-inflected, improvisational aesthetic, as jazz reflects a cosmopolitanism that Waldron positions as "a way of being in the world, a way of constructing an identity for oneself that is different . . . from the idea of belonging to or devotion to or immersion in a particular culture" (227–28). Additionally, cosmopolitanism focuses upon interactions with the world outside the home. Thus, as we shall see, the adult Suder's journey to the self begins with his abandonment of home.

As an adolescent, Suder's self-affirmation begins to develop through his love of Parker's "Ornithology" and through his love and respect for nature and the sense of renewal that it gives him; time spent in the natural world, albeit briefly, seems to lessen his blues. When his family and friends become too much to cope with, the solace that he finds at the pond near his home helps him buffet negative, external pressures weighing on his sense of self. His reverence for nature is in sharp contradistinction to his brother's disdain for it. Visits to the pond fascinate them but for different reasons. Martin likes to visit the pond in order "to pick birds off the telephone line," while Suder finds peace in simply "watching tadpoles" (12). Martin, notorious for shooting down sparrows near the pond, terrorizes Suder and often makes him an unwilling participant in the killings. Wracked with guilt, Suder tries to make amends by keeping the dead birds from becoming prey to scavengers. He collects the dead sparrows in a box (his first unconscious fascination with flight) that he initially keeps in his bedroom and then the garage. The birds initiate within him a fascination with flight that helps him cope with the blues brought on by his family's dysfunction.

According to critics, jazz is a mode of conversation that unites and separates the individual from the larger community. Ralph Ellison explains that

> For true jazz is an art of individual assertion within and against the group. Each true jazz moment . . . springs from a contest in which each artist challenges all the rest, each solo flight, or improvisation, represents . . . a definition of his identity: as individual, as member of the collectivity and as a link in the chain of tradition. (*Shadow and Act* 234)

Improvisation, as a formal aspect of jazz, urges and allows the musician, as if on a quest for new territory, to go places others might not venture. Generally speaking, the quest or journey revolves around one's need to arrive at a point of contentment or self-actualization outside of the group—all the while maintaining important ties to the group. The quest motif in African American literature parallels improvisation in the way many characters search for existential and physical freedom from societal strictures. The quest motif is at the heart of *Suder*.

In the novel, as an adult, Suder's blues ontology appears to have changed very little. In the narrative's present moments, the reader is witness to Craig Suder's confused and unhappy life. He is a thirty-two-year old baseball player whose marriage and career are failing miserably. As the novel progresses, the development of Suder's more positive sense of self as a (black) man continues as he gradually comes to understand that jazz is indeed life; his desire is to share his newfound source of inspiration and vitality with others.

Jazz improvisation defines Suder's adult life. Considering that jazz patently evolves from the blues, Suder's adult life begins with the blues element and is transformed into a jazz-inflected, improvised journey that aids him in his quest for self-actualization. In the first section of the novel that details his adult life, we learn that Suder's blues stem from his sexual impotency, his failure as a father and role model to his son, and his slumping baseball career. He laments his situation in an unmistakable blues fashion:

> I put my face back into my hands. I get up and walk out of the kitchen, through the bedroom, and into the bathroom. I stand in the shower for a long time with the water pounding my back. Things are bad. I can't make love to my wife, I can't run bases, and I couldn't get a hit if they was pitching me basketballs underhanded. And my kid hates me. To top it off, I got a bum leg that don't hurt. (18–19)

Throughout these lines preside a sense of "lack." Suder, in a bluesy mood, testifies to being a failure at everything significant in his life. He ends his confession with humor that symbolically allows him to "laugh to keep from crying" because, unlike when he was a child, he can now mask his frustration behind a nonexistent knee injury. It is other people's expectations of him, however, that underpin much of his grief. He laments: "This matter of expectation is really getting to me and I begin to have an identity crisis of sorts. I don't know if I'm Craig Suder the ballplayer, or Craig

Suder the husband, or Craig Suder the fellow talking to the fat Germans in the elevator" (43). Each expectation boxes him into rigid roles concerning (black) masculinity and manhood. For example, through much of the story, Thelma, his wife, focuses primarily on her sexual life with Suder. When he cannot perform sexually, she has no use for him. By symbolically reducing him to the worth of his penis, she effectively emasculates him. Lou Tyler, his coach, is only concerned with Suder's athletic prowess, as if this defines who he is as a (black) man. His son, Peter, worships his father as a strong, seemingly invincible athlete and will not accept him in any other way.

Suder's struggle with the suppression of his "true" self in these situations echoes Ralph Ellison's "black and blue" invisible man, who despondently claims the following:

> All my life I had been looking for something, and everywhere I turned someone tried to tell me what it was. I accepted their answers too, though they were often in contradiction and even self-contradictory. I was naïve. I was looking for myself and asking everyone except myself questions which I and only I could answer.[6] (*Invisible Man* 15)

To counter the effect of the blues, Suder frees himself from immediate external pressures by taking a literal and metaphorical flight away from baseball and his family. He quits both, and his flight begins to take on the measure of a jazz solo personified. Suder's flight from and transposition of the blues introduces the jazz element into the narrative. As LeRoi Jones explains in *Blues People: Black Music in White America* (1963), "Jazz should not be thought of as successor to blues, but as a very original music that developed out of, and was concomitant with, blues and moved off into its own path of development" (71). In other words, the blues seems to designate hopeful resignation, while jazz appears to emphasize movement and action to overcome that resignation. Through this quest, Suder adopts a "jazz lifestyle," which Alphonso Hawkins claims, "looks for creative, nontraditional means of living and devises these means" (xx). At any given moment, the performer can choose his approach to the music of life; this is what Suder does when the blues has given him no recourse and he turns more earnestly to jazz for inspiration.

Lou loosely plants the seed for Suder's improvisational quest when he tells him to get his act together on the field. Standing in the locker room after Suder performs terribly on the field, Lou tells him, "Truth of the matter is, Craig, that you have to straighten up and fly right" (5). Suder takes the words to heart; he becomes fascinated with flying again. While on the plane returning from an away game, he stares out of the window, sees a bird, and wishes he "could fly up high and all without the aid of a machine" (5).[7]

A significant moment in the narrative occurs when Suder's family discovers that he has been placed on the baseball team's "Disabled List." When neither his wife nor son can understand what is happening with Suder, they both turn away from him, leaving him even more depressed. The terrible state of his life, however, makes him remember a song he had forgotten he liked, Charlie Parker's "Ornithology." The song mesmerizes him so much that he listens "to this one song maybe a dozen times" and explains, "I can't get enough of it. I can't get past it and I'm really getting caught up in the saxophone solo and I get excited and decide to tackle Thelma" (29). Although at times the music sexually arouses Suder, the more telling response is his inability to simply "hear" it. He listens so intently that it becomes embedded in his soul. Whenever he sinks into a blue funk, he returns to the album. To Suder, the most moving part of "The Song" is the saxophone solo; he shares:

> I get to thinking about the saxophone solo on this here recording and noticing how things get built around one melody. Even when the melody ain't played at all, somehow it's there and it's waiting when the saxophone is finished singing. And that's just what that saxophone does, it sings. (36)

For the first time, Suder recognizes the freedom intrinsic to an improvised jazz solo. Whenever he has a minute to himself, he returns to what he now calls "The Song" (38). "Ornithology" moves Suder further to ponder flight. As with classic jazz bebop, the tempo is upbeat and like as Parker's solo flights in "Ornithology," it moves in a recursive direction full of positive energy. One result that spawns from Suder's revelation about the power of jazz is that he develops a symbiotic relationship with "Ornithology."

Introspectively, he becomes fascinated with flying. For example, his next moment of flight-fancy occurs when he walks out on one of his many arguments with Thelma and heads to the park to watch pigeons. The children mercilessly harass the birds and, fearing for their lives, they take flight. Likewise, at a bar with his friend David, Suder wants to play "The Song" but is thrown out because of his apparent "insanity" in daring to change the music already playing on the jukebox.

Frustrated with his family and friend's lack of understanding, he embarks on a journey to find himself. Before he leaves, however, he purchases an alto saxophone, the instrument that Charlie "Bird" Parker plays on "Ornithology." This act symbolizes his desire for freedom, as the saxophone marks the quintessential moment of improvisation in "Ornithology." In Suder's every encounter from here, we see the psychological transformation of a black man unhampered by the perplexities and difficulties of being "black" and "male" in society. Jazz awakens in him a desire for radical change.

When fully embarking on his flight of freedom, Suder realizes that he has left home so abruptly that he "ain't got no bucks to speak of" (66). In a bizarre encounter at a one-man circus, he is able to procure money in a sick game that involves physically abusing an elephant. Suder then encounters his old friend Sid with whom he boards for a few days in order to get his bearings. Sid, a character who has lived a very rough life, represents that which is antithetical to improvisation and freedom because he cannot move beyond white society's prescriptive notions surrounding his identity. Sid, a Narragansett Indian, is only allowed into the Major League as a token "black" ballplayer in order to refute the idea that all black baseball players are great athletes. In spite of his assertion of his Native American ethnic identity, whites see him as a "nigger" and laugh at his incompetency (Everett 83). However, he eventually turns out to be a great ballplayer, which undermines why the League hired him in the first place. Ironically displeased by his athletic prowess, the League releases him from his contract. Sid endures disparaging remarks about his identity and serves as a foil for Suder. He interacts very little with people and lives alone on a boat. Debauchery, womanizing, and petty crime define his existence, and he has no desire to rise above his vices.

Nevertheless, Sid travels from bar to bar with Suder, carrying his phonograph, his record, and his saxophone to spread the gospel of "Ornithology." However, most people, including Sid, find Suder's behavior strange, and summarily dismiss him as insane. Each time he enters a bar to play "The Song," the other patrons become irritated and demand that the music be turned off. They are not used to listening to jazz and its strange cadences are foreign to their sensibilities. They neither understand the music nor Suder. Their negative responses symbolize their misunderstanding of not only jazz but also the implicit freedom it provides Suder; their dismissive reaction only exacerbates Suder's desire to create an identity outside of prescribed perceptions of what jazz is and what (black) masculinity means for him. Thus far, Suder's quest has garnered him only derision and scorn, and he leaves Portland because of his mistreatment and because Sid threatens his life.

During his journey, Suder takes refuge at a boardinghouse where a group of Chinese gay men reside. He has no place to call home and decides that living in the boardinghouse is as good a place as any. His new living arrangement symbolizes his assuredness of his sexuality and his masculinity. It also symbolizes an improvisation on his former relationship with his family and friends. As an outsider, Suder feels more at ease with a group of Chinese gay men than he does with his family and friends. In fact, one of the men, Thomas, who is almost morbidly obese, is sexually attracted to Suder. However, Suder, who is aware of Thomas's feelings toward him, does not feel the least bit threatened. He treats Thomas as a friend and not as a pariah or someone who threatens his masculinity. His only desire is to initiate Thomas into the gospel of "Ornithology." He remains at the boardinghouse with Thomas until Sid arrives once again threatening Suder and demanding the money Suder had stolen from him. Sid almost kills him, but he manages to escape once more and continues on his journey. In the car that Thomas gives him, Suder thinks: "So, I'm driving through Portland in Thomas's station wagon . . . . There's a box of clear plastic bubbles with little toys inside on the seat beside me and in one of them there's an eye. The eye is staring right at me and I think of Sid and I think of fat Thomas's arms wrapped around him" (108). It is at this point in the novel that Suder begins to be able to laugh at the absurdity of his situation. The eye/"I" as metaphor represents his nascent awakening to how he must begin to envision his life, if he is to truly find himself.

Free and clear of Sid for now and sent off with glad tidings from Thomas, Suder once again encounters the elephant that he abused earlier on. However, the trainer has a new scam that requires Suder to succeed in making the elephant nod for "yes" and shake his head for "no" (109). This time, instead of inflicting pain upon the elephant to coerce him into doing his bidding, he accomplishes the feat by "whispering" to it; like Dr. Doolittle, he converses with the elephant. Suder shows him a baseball bat and

> I walk out in front of the elephant . . . and [its] eyes fall slowly to mine. The silence [from the crowd] is really annoying and I swallow. I raise the bat and wave it in the elephant's face. "Remember me?" I ask the elephant. The elephant's head moves up and down. The crowd goes "Ooooooooooo." I look around and the silence returns. I look back at the elephant. "Do you want me to do what I did last time?" The elephant moves his head from side to side and the mob of people explodes with cheering. I turn to face the carnival man. (109)

Suder's decision not to use violence to get the results he desires is significant here. The baseball bat, which he used to coerce the elephant in their previous encounter, is not needed. In the past, baseball was one of the things that defined him in his own eyes as well as in the eyes of others. The baseball bat is a phallic symbol, a signifier of power and his athletic and sexual prowess. In this instance, he recognizes that baseball is not the thing that defines him and that the power to define himself can only come from within. As Wei-ham Ho has written, jazz's "entire history has been the freeing of time, pitch, and harmony from fixed, regulated, predictable standards" (285). In other words, like a jazz musician, Suder begins to accept his newfound life on the fringes of society in earnest.

Indeed, Suder becomes so taken with the elephant that he successfully barters him away from its trainer. So now on this comic journey is a black man, his "Ornithology" record, a phonograph, a baseball bat, a few thousand dollars, a saxophone he has yet to competently learn how to play, and an elephant that he hauls around in a truck. The improvisational, carnavalesque journey is a comical highpoint in the novel; but despite the apparent absurdity of the situation, Suder is at his most serene. That *he* is the one who has made these spectacular and peculiar life-altering decisions is an impactful part of his spiritual and psychological journey.

As exhibited when he was a child, Suder, as an adult, is still drawn to the serenity of nature. It represents a spiritual site for him as he ponders what it means to be free. Thus, Suder seeks refuge in the quiet calm of the forest around Mount Hood, Oregon. He boards in Lou's vacation cabin, where he spends his time walking the elephant, now called "Renoir," and enjoying the sound of the saxophone on "Ornithology." When he is not playing the record, he attempts to play his saxophone, but with little success. Still, he soldiers on. While shopping in town for clothes, he witnesses a little white girl arguing with her mother. The little girl, whose narrative echoes Suder's, wants the freedom to choose what she will wear rather than the dresses that her mother picks out for her. Like him, the little girl seeks to assert her own individuality. However, the mother will not stand for her rebelliousness and slaps her twice. When he leaves the store, Suder finds that Jincy Jessy Jackson, the little girl from the store, has stowed away in his truck. Jincy wants to leave with Suder because her mother physically abuses her. Simultaneously alarmed and amused at her audacity, he allows her to accompany him back to the cabin, despite the serious repercussions of "kidnapping" a child.

At the cabin, Jincy, Renoir, and Suder happily coexist until the townspeople discover that Jincy is missing, along with bales of hay stolen from local farms to feed Renoir. Despite the danger of discovery, Suder becomes spiritually alive in nature. While on a walk in the woods with Renoir and Jincy, who is riding on the elephant's back, he once again discovers the sublimity of the pond and the beauty of an osprey's magnanimous flight above it. He is "really excited, watching the osprey fly off, his big wings beating. Then there's a loud high-pitched scream and I see this bald eagle. The osprey drops his fish and the eagle catches it, and I'm a little sickened by this. No wonder it's our national bird" (124). The eagle's attack on the osprey symbolizes the predatory nature of American society where might makes right. For Suder, the eagle does not symbolize freedom in America but its opposite: violence, brutality, and abuse of power.

Nevertheless, his desire to fly becomes even more pronounced. Every day, Suder walks out to Ezra Pond to observe the freedom symbolized by the osprey's flight. Moved completely by his serene environment and Parker's "Ornithology," Suder claims, "flying is a distinct possibility and that being a bird is well worth my while" (142). He understands the dangers of rigid classifications and catagorizations when one morning out in the woods he meets a zoologist, Richard Beckwith:

> "What are you looking at?" the zoologist asks.
> I point up at the bird.
> "Oh, *Haliaeetus leucocephalus*," he says, sitting beside me.
> "Bald eagle."
> "Pretty amazing, eh?"
> I look up at him and hoist up my eyebrows . . . .
> "I wish I could fly."
> He chuckles. "Wishes, wishes."
> I think I will. (139–40)

He gives up his attempts at playing the saxophone because it disturbs Jincy and Renoir; and instead, he learns to fly.[8] His journey has led him to profound self-reflection and self-acceptance as he claims, "Here I am, a black ballplayer in the mountains of Oregon with an elephant, a smart ass nine-year old white girl, and a black Indian tied up in my dead manager's cabin. And to top it all off, I'm planning to fly off a mountain. I laugh out loud" (155). His observation about his life at this point contrasts those from earlier in the novel. Before, he was in a blue funk created by others' perceptions and expectations. Here, he has defined himself based on the choices he has made up to this moment—a Nietzschean will to power. More importantly, with contentment, he releases a laugh of social defiance and self-approval. For Suder, flying is a life-affirming act.

At the end of the novel, we witness Suder's refiguration as a self-reliant (black) man who performs the most important event of his life with innovation, courage, and vision. After telling Jincy, "I want to be free," he builds an apparatus from dead bird feathers that allows him to become the "Bird" that Bud Powell had once called him, the "Bird" soaring in Charlie Parker's "Ornithology," and the literal bird that flies off Willet Rock. When Suder actually leaps off the rock, he struggles initially with his new skill but soon understands the mechanics of flying. As he soars above the lake, he imagines that the zoologist, Beckwith, has given him a Latin name to represent his species, *"homo sapien,"* as the people from below witness his flight. While Beckwith may indeed call him by this Latin name, Suder has final say as he simply asserts that he is, "Craig Suder" (171), with no appositives with which to define him. This naming, an act of validation through self-identification, represents his arrival to selfhood through which he experiences freedom and contentment. Through the improvisation of blues and jazz throughout *Suder*, we witness a (black) man's evolution from the defined to the definer.

Everett's appropriation of the blues and jazz motif in his first novel, *Suder*, affirms his inclusion in the African American literary tradition as it simultaneously affirms his rightful place in the American literary tradition. Even if as Russett argues, "Everett unhinges 'black' subject matter from lingering stereotypes of 'black' style, while challenging the assumption that a single or consensual African American experience exists to be represented" (360), his narrative strategy is in direct dialogue with his African American *and* American literary ancestors and contemporaries.[12] In *Suder*, Everett portrays an African American character who does not represent a monolithic African American experience. Instead, Suder's journey symbolizes a human experience, regardless of race; one that is marked by existential improvisation and experimentation. Nevertheless, *Suder also* sets the stage for what has arguably become one of Everett's literary missions: to liberate black men from the roles and stereotypes that society has created and prescribed. More specifically, he confronts racial and gender stereotypes that seek to define black men, like Craig Suder, who make the difficult choice to "finger the jagged grain" (Ellison, qtd. in Baker, 133). Suder's journey symbolizes a worldview where through resilience, spirituality, and interdependence the sky's the limit. Everett's critique and refiguration of the (black) male experience in this contemporary moment speaks to a mission carried out by other African American male writers who write against a long tradition of invisible men, native sons, and strangers in the village. Consequently, Everett recognizes that the rhythm of (black) humanity rests in improvisation, in which who you are and not what you are instantiates "flying home" to the frequencies of all that life has to offer.

Notes

1. Peter Monaghan provides an overview of Everett's career as a professor and writer. See "Satiric Inferno," *Chronicle of Higher Education*, February 11, 2005, A18+: Print.

2. Gene Andrew Jarrett's anthology, *African American Literature Beyond Race: An Alternative Reader* (2006), provides an alternative canon of African American writers whose work depicts characters who are white or racially unmarked. A number of Everett's novels, *Cutting Lisa* (1986), *Zulus* (1990), *Frenzy* (1997), and *American Desert* (2004), fit this category.

3. See note 1.

4. Literary critic Margaret Russett uses these specific terms to describe what she suggests are cultural markers of African American literature. See "Race under Erasure" in the works cited.

5. Kristen Henson's *Beyond the Sound Barrier: The Jazz Controversy in Twentieth-Century American Fiction* (2003) specifically examines the presence of jazz in American and African American fiction and how the genre impacted the culture from which it stemmed as well as the larger American culture. She explores jazz as a trope in James Weldon Johnson's *Autobiography of an Ex-Colored Man* (1912/1927), F. Scott Fitzgerald's general assertion of a "Jazz Age," Langston Hughes's *The Ways of White Folk* (1934), and Toni Morrison's *Jazz* (1992).

6. In Ellison's *Invisible Man* (1952), "The Prologue" reveals the narrator as a black man inundated with and suffering from the blues. To create mood in this section, Ellison signify(s) on trumpeter Louis Armstrong's seminal blues song, "What Did I Do to Be So Black and Blue," which was originally composed in 1929 by Fats Waller. Everett also invokes this narrative strategy to help convey the protagonist of the novel, Craig Suder's blues.

7. Flying is a quintessential metaphor for freedom in modern and contemporary African American literature, music, and art. See Richard Wright's *Native Son* (1940), Ralph Ellison's short story, "Flying Home," Ishmael Reed's *Flight to Canada* (1976), and even Toni Morrison's male-centered novel, *Song of Solomon* (1977).

8. I would argue that Suder gives up playing the saxophone because he realizes that he is using the music that he loves, Parker's "Ornithology," to try to indoctrinate other people to view life his way. In this regard, jazz becomes another sign of conformity and not individual expression and freedom.

Chapter 7

"Do you mind if we make Craig Suder white?"

From Stereotype to Cosmopolitan to Grotesque in Percival Everett's Suder

ANTHONY STEWART

> He wondered, as he had many times wondered before whether he himself was
> a lunatic. Perhaps a lunatic was simply a minority of one. At one time it has
> been a sign of madness to believe that the earth goes round the sun: today, to
> believe that the past is unalterable. He might be *alone* in holding that belief,
> and if alone, then a lunatic. But the thought of being a lunatic did not greatly
> trouble him: the horror was that he might also be wrong.
>
> —GEORGE ORWELL, *Nineteen Eighty-Four*

Nobody writes about *Suder*.[1] Percival Everett's first novel, published in
1983, seems to attract less critical attention than the rest of his considerable body of work, and this is quite an assertion when taking into account
how little critical attention his work receives in general. The reasons for
this novel having been overlooked probably come down to its apparent
formalistic modesty when compared to the pyrotechnical virtuosity of
Glyph (1999), *Erasure* (2001), *American Desert* (2004), and *The Water Cure*
(2007), for instance. Even when I teach Everett's fiction, nobody decides
to write his or her term paper on *Suder*. All of this is a shame, because an
understanding of *Suder* helps us understand much of the rest of Everett's
oeuvre. Its position as his first novel emphasizes this foundational importance all the more. For instance, the mechanisms by which individuals
are rendered as stereotypes are critiqued throughout *Suder*. In itself, this
is not surprising, since much of Everett's work attacks the ways in which
categories are formed and—more problematically—become conventional

and, as a result, habitually unexamined. More interesting with respect to *Suder* are the title character's strategies for resisting being rendered as a stereotype. These strategies, what they promise to teach about Everett's work, and how we might rethink our conventional ways of viewing the "Other," focus this paper.

Stereotyping and cosmopolitanism make logical and appropriate complements in a discussion of *Suder*, since both are responses to one's coming into contact with—or at the very least awareness of—someone who is unlike oneself. As Homi Bhabha makes clear, stereotyping, irrespective of its cause, requires not openness but a closed mind, which he describes as a desire for "fixity":

> Fixity, as the sign of cultural/historical/racial difference in the discourse of colonialism, is a paradoxical mode of representation: it connotes rigidity and an unchanging order as well as disorder, degeneracy and daemonic repetition. Likewise the stereotype, which is its major discursive strategy, is a form of knowledge and identification that vacillates between what is always "in place," already known, and something that must be anxiously repeated . . . as if the essential duplicity of the Asiatic or the bestial sexual licence of the African that needs no proof, can never really, in discourse, be proved. (66)[2]

The need to reiterate the stereotype makes all the more patent its eventual conventionality. Reiteration leads to habit. Habit becomes easier to leave unexamined.

Kwame Anthony Appiah describes the notion of cosmopolitanism as follows: "cosmopolitanism shouldn't be seen as some exalted attainment: it begins with the simple idea that in the human community, as in national communities, we need to develop habits of coexistence: conversation in its older meaning, of living together, association" (xix). "Habits of coexistence" sound very promising when compared to the desire for and imposition on others of fixity. Replacing one set of habits with what appear at first to be a more progressive set of habits looks like improvement. However, Appiah acknowledges underlying threats to this potentially progressive set of new behaviors: "We enter every conversation—whether with neighbors or with strangers—without a promise of final agreement"

(44). In other words, there are no guarantees that cosmopolitanism will lead necessarily to political progress.

The conflict between fixity and conversation, then, results in logical incongruities that are ideological (i.e., constructed), and seem natural, but which actually require close scrutiny. This conflict resides in the history of Everett's first novel itself, as he tells the story of an offer from Norman Lear's Embassy Pictures to option the film rights to *Suder*. As Everett writes in his 1991 essay, "Signing to the Blind":

> *Suder* is a novel about an African-American's internal search for emancipation. Craig Suder is obsessed and terrified by the craziness of his mother, an insanity which is a metaphor for the American experience as she is taunted by white religion which fights her own attempt to find freedom. This is a novel about an African-American shedding the baggage of America and yet the first question put to me was, "Do you mind if we make Craig Suder white?" (9)

Everett's foray into the world of motion pictures (the movie is not made) points up a twice-over failing of cosmopolitanism on the part of Embassy Pictures. First, they fail to imagine Suder as the compelling African American subject that he is, a failing reflective of much of North American popular culture. Second, they fail even to imagine an *audience* who might be able to imagine Suder as the compelling African American subject that he is, irrespective of the race of individual audience members.

But there is an additional dimension to the failure of Embassy Pictures as regards Everett's novel, which must be mentioned in light of the nature of the novel itself. *Suder* is, in addition to an internal search for emancipation, a test of the title character's abilities to converse across boundaries and, in the face of a failure of conversation, to find emancipation in some other way. The novel is in fact replete with examples of this test and the various successes and failures of characters in the face of this test. It represents multiple attempts at such conversations: black/white, male/female, representative/individual, technical/vernacular, stereotype/cosmopolitan, sane/insane, and the binary that perhaps contains these others: conventional/unconventional. I will not attempt to engage systematically with all of these boundaries here, because to resolve such binaries is, ultimately, not the constructive point toward which Everett's work leads us. Instead, I will describe a trajectory that works its way through the novel as Suder intuits his stereotyped subjectivity and attempts to escape this position first by becoming cosmopolitan, but then, finally and successfully, by becoming "grotesque," as Leonard Cassuto uses this term, defining the tension created in the space between categories. It is in this space that Suder decides to live and in which Everett creates.

The fraught relationship between the representative and the individual introduces the notion of the stereotype to the novel. Craig Suder is introduced as a third baseman for the Seattle Mariners who is suffering through a hitting slump. To make matters worse, he is also enduring a bout of sexual impotence. His manager, Lou Tyler, tells him after yet another subpar game: "Now, about that slump of yours. You know, it wasn't but a few years ago that you blacks was allowed in this league. The way you been playing lately, they might kick you all out" (25). Later, Suder, reflecting upon his increasing inability to make himself understood by others, thinks to himself: "maybe people can't listen and understand if they're busy expecting things of me. This matter of expectations is really getting to me and I begin to have an identity crisis of sorts. I don't know if I'm Craig Suder the ballplayer, or Craig Suder the husband, or Craig Suder the fellow talking to the fat Germans in the elevator" (43). This sense of dislocation emphasizes the stress of occupying the position of the stereotype. Under the limiting pressure of expectations, expressions of cosmopolitanism stand as a welcome respite by contrast.

The logical absurdities of stereotyping appear in high relief in a conversation between Suder and a former baseball player, Sid Willis, who tells the story of his own entrance into and then dismissal from the world of major league baseball. Willis says that he never really enjoyed playing in the majors because he resented the reason he was allowed into the major leagues in the first place: "Well, when I started there wasn't but four or five blacks playing in the big leagues and they was all excellent—Jackie Robinson, Satchel Paige, and like that. And they brought me in because they was looking for a darky that wasn't so good . . . I guess they figured they had to show that dark folks could be bad, too. I mean, every black playing was great and then came Sid Willis, Mr. Below Average" (83). Of course, with this logic in place, it stands to reason that the inevitable happens to Willis: "Then one season things just fell into place and I was hitting like three-fifty and they let me go . . . Because all of a sudden I was another excellent dark-skinned ballplayer" (83). It's important that the story is amusing, ridiculous even, and—given the logic that underlies it—troublingly plausible. Willis's individual success can only logically be held against him. The black player has to be representative; he cannot participate as an individual on his own terms. In effect, he is a visitor, "allowed" to play because of the largesse of others who do not see him for himself and need him to do their ideological bidding. He must also always represent quite specific things. In Willis's case, the purpose he serves is to mollify the animosity of those presumably white members of the ticket-buying public who might resent the skills of other baseball players who superficially resemble him. Strictly speaking, Willis's job is to represent a comforting exception that disproves the apparent rule. He is to embody black baseball incompetence. Once he no longer serves this palliative function when his slump ends he is completely expendable.

This pressure to represent the group to which one happens to belong has—obviously—a very long history, although it is usually recounted in quite dire tones, instead of the often humorous or absurd tones employed by Everett. Todd, in Ralph Ellison's story, "Flying Home," for instance, says: "Now the humiliation would come. When you must have them judge you, knowing that they never accept your mistakes as your own but hold it against your whole race—that was humiliation" (150). More recently, the same abject sense of this injustice is characterized by Lisa Baird, then a columnist for the Bergen County *Record*, who wrote a column in response to Colin Ferguson's 1993 shooting spree on a Long Island Rail Road train. She writes that in addition to the horror of the event, for some "the initial fluttering was accompanied by a prayer: 'Lord, please don't let him be black'" (160). My point here is not about the injustice itself but that Everett portrays this injustice in the form of a joke, with Willis eventually delivering the punch line: "And I ain't even black" (83). He's a Narragansett Indian, so this desire to stereotype is rendered explicitly ludicrous (as it always is implicitly) by his misidentification by the cognizing audience. Nevertheless, he still serves the same ideological purpose because he is dark skinned. The sense of the unfair pressure imposed upon a member of a minoritized group is perhaps more palpable through Everett's humorous rendition of it, rather than conventionally more dire versions. In fact, this presentation suggests all the more clearly the same inability of some to see beyond their preexisting and limiting ideas, as was the case with Embassy Pictures and the prospective film version of *Suder*.

Craig Suder, of course, is all too aware of his own expendability. In response to the pressure of being stereotyped, Suder tries to turn himself into something else. His first attempt is to become a cosmopolitan who can converse across boundaries. But recasting oneself as a cosmopolitan is no easy task. Remember Appiah's caution that cosmopolitanism does not necessitate "a promise of final agreement." Nor is it a fail-safe solution to the problem of being cast in a fixed role.

It is here that we encounter another of the pairings mentioned earlier, between the sane and the insane. Suder has a justifiable fear of being insane as a result of his mother's often-bizarre behavior when he was a child. He describes this scene from his childhood: "I had plans to visit the pond and when I walked into the kitchen I found Ma at the counter, stirring the contents of a bowl and running in place. She was wearing her heavy coat and a brand-new pair of black high-top sneakers. Perspiration was pouring off her face and the fur about her collar looked matted in places" (22). As we eventually discover, his mother's compulsive running while wearing a heavy coat is caused by her insecurity that her husband is having an affair. As she haltingly says to her bewildered young son: "Running . . . to lose weight . . . Lou Ann . . . Narramore . . . skinny . . . lose weight . . ." (22). This part makes sense, but one cannot help but speculate upon the effect of such a spectacle on a small boy. As well, as it turns out, Kathy Suder's actions are just paranoia on her part, since her husband is not having an affair. In fact, he barely knows the woman under suspicion. The fragmented manner in which she explains herself partly reflects, no doubt, the exertion of speaking while running in place. In addition, however, it makes clear Kathy's lacking of a vocabulary to convey her worries intelligibly to her family, and so instead she manifests them in extreme physical terms. She, too, is trying to converse across boundaries, and is incapable of doing so, in part because her family members have already decided that she is "crazy," and can only interpret what she says based on that assumption.

She has become fixed in their view, irrespective of her attempts to recast herself.

With this image of Suder's mother and his anxieties about the possibly hereditary nature of insanity, the challenge of finding a vocabulary that conveys one's thoughts, desires, and values to others is heavily freighted and an important recurring theme in *Suder*. This is not surprising when considering questions related to cosmopolitanism. As Appiah notes: "Like all vocabulary, evaluative language is primarily a tool we use to talk to one another, not an instrument for talking to ourselves. You know what you call someone who uses language mostly to talk to himself? Crazy" (28). Suder, then, is moving directly into the heart of his own anxiety. His expression of his own vocabulary manifests itself in behavior that looks as "crazy" as his mother's, finding its first expression in his obsession with Charlie Parker's composition, "Ornithology." But as Appiah says, vocabularies are modes of communication with others, which is exactly what Suder tries to do. It is not enough for him to be moved by Parker's song. His most extreme, but by no means his only, attempt to get others to listen to "Ornithology" occurs when he goes to a jazz club, along with a casual acquaintance named Thomas, to hear Dizzy Gillespie play:

> Thomas and I are sitting at a table against the wall, far away from the band, and Dizzy walks out and starts to play. They play a long version of "A Night in Tunisia" and then I start shouting, "'Ornithology'! 'Ornithology'!" Dizzy begins to play the song and I fall back into my chair with a smile across my face. My hand drops down next to me and lands on my saxophone and I decide to join in. So, I stand up and start blowing and Thomas is looking around nervously and Dizzy stops playing. (99)

Part of his compulsion with "Ornithology" has been his taking up (as in: picking up to carry around, not "taking up" as in to learn) the saxophone, which is always with him in his peregrinations through the novel after he is put on extended leave by the Mariners.

Thomas's nervousness in this scene is completely understandable, Suder's behavior much less so. Suder wants Gillespie to appreciate *his* playing the way Suder does. But, of course, he cannot. No one can. Suder mistakes cosmopolitanism as conversation for self-determination as imposition, the sort of old-fashioned application of cosmopolitanism that enabled well-traveled and well-heeled citizens from colonizing nations to travel the world and try to "civilize" those they met on their travels, not to understand others on their own terms—to convert rather than to converse. Appiah accounts for this old-fashioned version of cosmopolitanism by beginning his book with a discussion of Sir Richard Francis Burton, the Victorian adventurer who "is a standing refutation, then, to those who imagine that prejudice derives only from ignorance, that intimacy must breed amity. You can be genuinely engaged with the ways of other societies without approving, let alone adopting, them" (9). This is who Suder has become by this point in the novel. Cosmopolitanism is not, in and of itself, an answer to his stereotyping. The example of Burton points out that cosmopolitanism is no guarantee of open-mindedness or, for that matter, progress. There remains the same mechanism operating within any enactment of cosmopolitanism that operates within the desire for fixity—that is, the limits of the human imagination.

Toward the middle of the novel, another jazz legend, Bud Powell, hints at the distinction between this type of old-fashioned cosmopolitanism and the more self-determinative resolution that Suder seeks. Powell is a friend of Suder's father when Craig is a child, and cannot help but notice Kathy Suder's peculiar behavior, as everyone does. But Powell's assessment distinguishes itself from that of the rest of the family: "He said that maybe Ma was just different. I was searching for 'just different' in the woman dashing back and forth, back and forth, but all I saw was crazy" (82). It is important that it takes someone from outside the family to revise Kathy's behavior to them. Powell exhibits a progressive cosmopolitan willingness to approve of—or at least accept—Kathy on her own terms. He brings a different language to the family's habitual practices and is able to reinterpret these practices as a result. He doesn't convert; he converses. Commenting on the stereotyping pressure exerted upon African American writers, Everett observes in "Signing to the Blind": "I do not believe that the works we produce need to be any different; the failing is not in what we show but in how it is seen. And it is not just white readers, but African-American readers as well who seek to fit our stories to an existent model. It is not seeing with 'white' eyes, it is seeing with 'American' eyes, with brainwashed, automatic, comfortable, and 'safe' perceptions of reality" (10). Everett's words contextualize what Powell offers in his explanation of Kathy Suder's behavior—a perspective that frees the viewer from the impulse to fit the story to an existent model. Once his attempt at finding some form of cosmopolitan freedom through conversation fails, Suder must find some alternative, and it is here that the novel makes its most profound point, the point that is so suggestive of Everett's aesthetic more generally.

Seyla Benhabib, in her accounts of the "headscarf affair" in France and a change to German voting laws to accommodate recent immigrants,[3] writes that: "These cases show that outsiders are not only at the borders of the polity but also within it. In fact, the very binarism between nationals and foreigners, citizens and migrants is sociologically inadequate and the reality is much more fluid, as many citizens are of migrant origin, and many nationals themselves are foreign-born" (68). Benhabib's point about the fluidity of identity and the inadequacy of conventional binaries stands in stark contrast to the fixity desired in stereotyping, and finds a useful expression in Leonard Cassuto's conception of the grotesque, central to which is the notion of tension: "This tension is the unique and specific tension of the grotesque, the anomalous embodiment of cultural anxiety. The grotesque is born of the violation of basic categories. It occurs when an image cannot be easily classified even on the most fundamental level: when it is both one thing and another, and thus neither one" (6). So, while Benhabib gestures toward a cosmopolitan imperative to see others within as broad a context as possible, as well as to see ourselves in a similarly expansive way, this sense of expansiveness is facilitated if we remember how complex and multivalent each of us is, as opposed to allowing ourselves such complexity while rendering the "other" as fixed. Suder's contestation of his own stereotyping, which initially leads him to the conversation of cosmopolitanism, leads ultimately to a more radical self-expression, a destination that enables not only the critique of the stereotype but also draws attention to the inadequacies of cosmopolitanism. Having had his fill of being seen only as a black baseball player—in other words, being seen on others' most limited terms—and of being misunderstood in his attempts to converse, Suder decides that the most thoroughgoing escape from such limitations is to take to the air, to momentarily become something entirely different.

As Cassuto also argues: "By trying to imagine people as nonhuman, the objectifier opens a Pandora's box and releases the grotesque. The problems that result are such that the simple presence of the objectified (and therefore grotesque) other will unbalance the edifice of asserted difference" (33). Cassuto's conception of the grotesque highlights that stereotyping necessarily leads to the grotesque, since no one's identity is fixed as the reductive impulse to stereotype would have it. His image of the "release" of the grotesque could not describe the conclusion to *Suder* any more aptly, since Craig Suder's attempt to violate the repressive categories that have so long imprisoned and haunted him forces him to eschew the social demands of cosmopolitanism in favor of becoming something that only Craig Suder can become—namely, a man who flies like a bird.

Another of the conventional binaries violated by Everett's novel—here, the familiar versus the unfamiliar—is given voice in Suder's decision to reject the cosmopolitan/conversational approach for the grotesque when he provides a textbook structuralist answer to Sid Willis, who cannot get over the fact that Suder—during his travels—has acquired an elephant (whom Suder has named Renoir) as a pet:

> "What's that?" He points to Renoir with his head.
> "That's an elephant," I says.
> "Why?"
> I'm puzzled and I'm looking at Renoir. "Cause he ain't a dog." (153)

This answer is a clear gesture toward moving in other than the conversational direction suggested by cosmopolitanism.

Richard Beckwith, a zoologist, who joins the proceedings late in the novel, presents another opportunity to understand Suder's strategy for self-determination. Beckwith's habit is to pronounce the latinate name of every animal he sees. He says *"Loxodonta africana,"* and Suder says, "Elephant" (144). Suder's refusal to play by the rules of taxonomy Beckwith tries to impose upon him signals the shift in Suder's quest, from one of understanding to one of grotesque autonomy. As his resolve strengthens,

Suder begins to do what he feels is necessary to become closer to bird-like: he starts to eat worms, he tries to raise his body temperature by deliberately catching a cold, and attempts to increase the flexibility of his neck (having been told of the extreme flexibility of avian spines). The crucial point here is not that he expects to *become* a bird, but that he approaches asymptotically the category of "bird," heightening our realization of his violation of the basic categories, a violation upon which he begins to thrive. Once Suder begins to understand his desire to fly, he expresses a sense of autonomy and purpose he lacks before coming to this realization.

The nature of Craig Suder's escape from the limitation imposed upon him by others finds expression in Everett's 2007 novel, *The Water Cure*. Ishmael Kidder, the novel's tormented narrator, reflects during one of his breaks from the narrative proper on the infinite nature of the space between categories:

What is between you and your first reflection? Space? The glass of the mirror? That which makes the glass a mirror? You know, you never ever touch or even face the thing that stands in opposition to you, only that which is between you and that thing. You only have experience with the between. But if the between is the thing to which you attend, then what is between you and the between? And what is the between between the betweens? Zeno, Zeno, Zeno. The number of points between here and the moon is infinite. The number of points between you and the door is infinite. Infinity equals infinity, and so the door is as far away as the moon. Still, if we both started walking right now, together, at the same time, I'd make it to the moon before you made it to that door. (46)

What Kidder is describing is the infinitude of the grotesque, the liberation of the potentially infinite space between categories. It is in this space that Craig Suder finally decides he would like to live. Once we understand this about Suder (and about *Suder*), we get a long way toward understanding what is available in Everett's aesthetic.

Margaret Russett has written of the endings of Everett's texts: "Often cryptic or abrupt, sometimes dissonant, Everett's conclusions spurn closure to the point of eliciting aesthetic dissatisfaction" (364); and while it

is true that his novels tend to be cryptic in their conclusions, I am arguing that the conclusion of *Suder*, at least, is completely satisfying, once we
recognize its purpose. Once his preparations are complete (and his plastic
wings are fashioned, lined with birds' feathers), he leaps off Willett Rock:
"I free-fall for about fifty feet with my wings doing everything except what
I want them to do and I pee because I'm scared and all of a sudden I'm
gliding" (171). As this climactic scene continues, Suder's exhilaration in
his accomplishment only increases: "I'm feeling the wind on my face and
listening to it roaring past my ears and I've got an erection. And I'm flying,
god-damnit, I'm flying" (171). Beckwith stands and watches Suder's flight
and provides the opportunity for the ultimate declaration of Suder's accomplishment, articulated by Suder himself:

> Then I see Beckwith on a ridge with the hunters and he's pointing
> up at me. I imagine him to say, "Homo sapiens."
> And I says, "Craig Suder." (171)

This terminal flourish defines Suder on his own terms, as it's fair to say
that he is the only man—black or not—in the world living in a cabin in
the woods with a nine-year-old white girl whom he has rescued from her
abusive mother, who owns an elephant as a pet, and is, at this moment,
flying with the aid of plastic wings lined with bird feathers.

In the face of the pressure of being stereotyped, perhaps the answer
is not the turning of the other cheek approach of the cosmopolitan but
an assertion of the aggressive and radical autonomy available in the grotesque. At this point he is not "too black" or "not black enough"; the in-
eptitude of his performance does not threaten the livelihood of others
who happen to resemble him superficially. He is only Craig Suder, and this
is his great accomplishment. As he flies over the group of people watching
from the ground, to say anything else about who he is can only miss the
point.

The escape into the grotesque may appear as a utopian fantasy only possible in art, and perhaps not even there, as Everett's experience with Embassy Pictures makes abundantly clear. However, the contribution that Everett's first novel makes to how we consider the categories through which
we view our world lies in its requirement that we interrogate our habitual

interpretations. One need not be able to take flight like a bird to be able to commit oneself to questioning the associations we tend to make through habit. Habits are, after all, difficult to unlearn, but this unlearning must be easier than learning how to fly.

Notes

1. With apologies to Jacqueline Berben-Masi, whose article, "Getting to First Base: Baseball as Organizing Metaphor in *Suder*," is the only other essay on *Suder* that I am aware of.

2. I have employed Bhabha's formulation regarding fixity as the underlying desire of stereotyping elsewhere. See "Cooperation in the Face of Defection: The Prisoner's Dilemma in *Invisible Man*," *Nebula* 4, no. 2 (June 2007): 183–207. In that essay, I also briefly address the distinction Leonard Cassuto makes between the Bhabha notion of hybridity and his own notion of the grotesque, both ideas that come up later in a different application in this essay.

3. Benhabib observes: "A consequence of transformation of citizenship is the long- and short-term coexistence of individuals and groups belonging to distinct and often quite contradictory cultures, mores and norms in the same public space" (51). She makes her argument with an account of *"L'affaire du foulard,"* the 1989 controversy in France initiated by the expulsion of three Muslims girls from their schools for wearing head scarves. She discusses a similar set of challenges to conventional interpretations of national citizenship in Germany in 1989 and 1990, in which rules governing participation in local municipal and district-wide elections were changed (62).

Chapter 8

Charting the Body

Percival Everett's Corporeal Landscapes in re: f (gesture)

SARAH WYMAN

Percival Everett's poems celebrating the body in *re: f (gesture)* (2006) refresh our perceptions and revel in the semantic and sonic impact of language even as they upset our expectations. Instead of communicating meaning in the transparent ways we may anticipate, Everett's poems figure forth fragments of familiar phenomena (a sternum, a tongue), in ways rendering them almost unrecognizable. Each mystified object, the depicted bodily bit, each poem itself, functions as an autonomous sign, free from standard communication, and thus freed as far as possible from culturally marked constructions. Through techniques of defamiliarization, the body meets us in an aestheticized version, rendered in a verbal medium that insists we take a second look in our effort to understand. The poetic voice seems to speak in an intimately individual way, yet presents us with universal facts of human form and experience that dismantle categorical boundaries between us.

As poet-painter, novelist, and wood-carver, Everett moves smoothly and skillfully between various modes of creativity and expression. As an artist well versed in language, paint, and wood, he investigates the relation between linguistic and formal structure and the production of meaning. As a scholar, he studies the play of signification, as words and paint splotches gesture toward meaning, as sounds and felt forms suggest sense to the one who reads, views, or touches. His poems become paintings of sorts, neat squares of eight lines, like his minimalist and highly abstracted paintings that invite our interpretive commentary.

These poems in *re: f (gesture)* venture into questions of representation as clearly as they query the minute workings of the human body. Even when we can identify the particular body part depicted in each poem, the text's effort at *ostranenie*, or "making strange,"¹ leads us beyond the mere task of labeling objects. Readerly focus shifts from simple decoding—"Oh, he's talking about an ear!"—to the way we can know an ear via a carefully engineered perceptual process. By controlling our visual consumption of the object, in the manner of a crafty cinematographer, Everett renews our experience of the world. By involving us in the meaning-making process of the ostensibly *writerly* text, he demands that we work harder as readers.² His riddles result in a new appreciation of the body as biological masterpiece and as a vehicle for physical and psychological connection. For example, the hyoid bone literally supports speech (43), as Everett puns on the structural relation between tongue and jaw. As art objects, each poem presents aestheticized language, capitalizing on connotation as often as denotation, and suggesting the human form as uncultured artifact.

With a sort of Flaubertian micro-vision, the poetic eye approaches the body, both its own male version and its other's female one. We zoom in on one aspect (the brain, the larynx, the inner ear), which becomes at once a landscape to travel, an object to turn in the hand, a source of scent, and a pathway to union with the world and other bodies. In an interview with Anthony Stewart, Everett speaks of artists as having a necessarily "narrow vision," just trying to paint a *piece* of the whole world.³ In a minimalist version of the traditional blazon, the poetic voice pieces together a form from parts of the body, fragment by fragment. Instead of a dismembering or objectification of the female form, however, one finds a building up through precise, chiseled details. The act of naming itself, with the accompanying savor of sound, signals value enough, without the intrusion of culturally marked qualifications of beauty. The nineteen poems in *re: f (gesture)* coalesce into a composite view of the body as idea, even medium: his/hers, mine/yours, inside/outside. As though quoting Russian Formalist Viktor Shklovsky directly, Everett feels that what matters "is not in what we show but in how it is seen" (Stewart 298). Although the artist claims that the subject (the human body) is secondary, the facts of embodied perception and identity prove paramount to broader questions of the cultured self.

The book cover, illustrated with Everett's own oil-on-canvas painting of a female nude, invites attention to the intersection of word and image, of linguistic and performative sign (figure 1). The truncated torso mirrors the shape of the italicized *f*, thus destabilizing easy divisions between visual and verbal signification. The minimalism of the painted form echoes the cryptic notation of the title with its abbreviated *re*, and implied *f*-word. The infinitely interpretable *(gesture)* both speaks its sonic flourish, free of heavy-handed semantics, and evokes an emphatically missing movement of the body. The visually rendered body simultaneously stands monolithically on absent legs, and seems to fall backward. Contextualized within anisotropic space, gravity grounds the figure. As in each of the *(Body)* poems, the painting presents us with something like a blank page, with partially tinted emphasis that serves to pull us in, beyond the surface layer of the skin. This painted body seems sculpted in stone, indexed as female via the curve of breast.

The cover painting's title, *The Wall*, specified nowhere in the book, introduces notions of division and difference so central to both Everett's poetic themes and his concerns as a structuralist scholar.[4] A wall both conjoins rooms and acts as a limit between them. Likewise, the body allows for the cleavage between individuals through touch and penetration, yet establishes individual autonomy as well. The painting's title again emphasizes the solid monumentality of the female torso and suggests both a keeping out and a possibility for entering in. As concrete object, the *body as wall* suggests notions of the phenomenal world that the poet will approach not with the scientific/positivist strategies his diction may suggest, but instead with a more playful deconstruction of typical ways we define the world through speech. Despite the quasi- clinical approach, an overriding tone of empathy suggests an intersubjective attitude in which the other is taken as a subject in itself rather than as an object among many.[5] The poetic voice ventures into words and sound units to probe the reality we experience only through the language that mediates our sensual experience.

The trope of the wall or limit perfectly introduces Everett's concerns with differential meaning and the play of signification. Stewart recalls in an interview, "You did say before that maybe what holds it all together is the line between signifier and the signified." Everett responds, "Well,

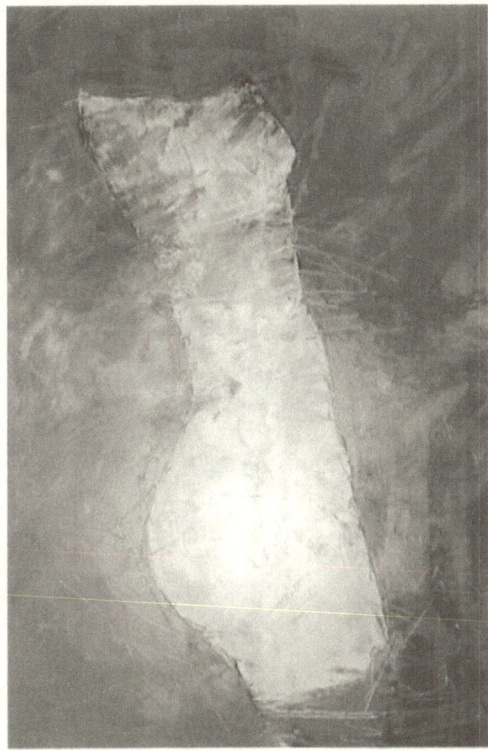

Figure 1. "The Wall" by Percival Everett. Credit: *The Wall*, 1985, by Percival Everett, Oil on canvas, 48" x 60", Collection of Francesca Rochberg, Reproduced by Permission of Percival Everett.

philosophically, that's what interests me. Trying to understand how that line between the meaning that we might intend and the meaning that we do perceive or receive, how that line at once divides it and holds it together" (296). Everett both describes the creative act of expression (in language, paint, wood) and alludes to the human act of communication (in words, gestures, other signs). Acknowledging discrepancies between intended meaning on the sender's end and (mis)interpretation on the receiver's end, Everett accepts and even embraces the imperfection of human efforts to express and to understand.

Thus, the intentional difficulty of Everett's poems on the body, the obscurity of the latinate language, the unexpected approach or perspective he takes on some less familiar aspect of the body, his lack of interest in establishing individual identities, all figure into broader philosophical questions for the poet. In his most famous novel, *Erasure* (2001), the same theme of *meaning* arises:

It's incredible that a sentence is ever understood. Mere sounds strung together by some agent attempting to mean some thing, but the meaning need not and does not confine itself to that intention. Those sounds, strung as they are in their peculiar and particular order, never change, but do nothing but change. Even if grammatical recognitions are crude, meaning is present. Even if the words are utterly confusing, there is meaning. Even if the semantic relationships are only general or categorical. Even if the language is unknown. Meaning is internal, external, orbital, but still there is no such thing as propositional content. Language never really effaces its own presence, but creates the illusion that it does in cases where meaning presumes a first priority. (*Erasure* 44)

Approaching the poems, then, one can feel free to experience them as aesthetic entities, as ventures in language and sound, in vision and thrust of feeling. The body becomes in effect, more a multivalent, abstract theme than an object of representation or subject of study.

Many of these *(Body)* poems initially appear in Everett's novel *Glyph* (1999). In this manifestation, a baby, then toddler, Ralph, voices the poems in a sort of stream of consciousness manner. Fully literate, well versed in critical theory, and abducted for most of the narrative due to his unusual intelligence, Ralph muses from his crib or his kidnapper's hip on language and on the adult drama transpiring around him. Ralph puzzles over the question of whether he is indeed a genius, or simply far too advanced to fit his infant body in a seemly way. Contextualized as pediatric utterings in *Glyph*, the poems differ in *re: f (gesture)* as they are written in the voice of an adult lover. For example, in *Glyph*, three lines of the poem "Larynx" recall a dear mother's cooing (112), whereas in *re: f (gesture)*, "it whispers, it calls, it cries, it makes those sounds" (55) now gathered on a single line, evoke an erotic moan. Everett's attention to formal and contextual transformations has given us paired poems of identical title that prove same and different at once.

Despite the deceptively clear form of the *(Body)* poems, neat four-stanza stacks of unrhymed couplets, these poems perplex the reader. Their very brevity often begs more information. Words themselves, like body parts, are determined within context. That which "braces" both abstract words and tangible tongue reveals itself as the horseshoe-shaped *hyoid bone*, once the poem's entire contexture unfolds through the time of reading. Due to categorical distinctions that unite opposites as surely as they divide them, such as I/you, he/she, inside/outside (47), a dialectic pull motivates most of these poems. The poet creates parallel tensions on various levels including the sense of directionality in opposition, writing "backward, downward" in "Obturator Internus," or "upward, inward" in the poem that follows, "Fissure of Sylvius." In "Obturator Internus," the voice contrasts dynamism and stasis, staging a kinetic drama of "arising," "descending," and "thrusting," all taking place within the still cavity of the pelvis (49). The *(Body)* poems exploit the juncture between same and different, combining versions of the seam or gap from the cranial fissures of Sylvus (50) and Rolando (58) to the genital fissure of the beloved (58). Through the device of accumulation, these physical features are presented as similar as though to foil the more striking differences between them. Speech becomes then, another gesture, pointing to, waving at semantic possibilities without committing in a positive way.

On the linguistic level as well, Everett plays with dialectic tensions from chiastic structures of language to other internally echoing sonic features. In "Labia Majora," sounds reflect around a y axis in an example of chiastic mirroring, "Posteriorly lost": ost – l – y – l – ost (l. 1). The iambic tetrameter of the line "the tongue she tells me she loves near" lulls with an assonance of long *ee* sounds punctuated by the alliterative *t*s (l. 7 "The Fissure of Rolando" 58). In the Structuralist tradition, language undermines any pretense of truth or presence by calling attention to itself as linguistic medium for play rather than a transparent window on meaning. In Everett's opinion, this play becomes the *only* truth we can count on. As he explains to Jim Kincaid, "Art is as close as we get to truth" (Kincaid 377). Thus, the poet does not put much stock in non-artistic cultural definitions of identity and reality.

Everett's poems function, indeed, as elaborate sound-scapes. He considers sounds (not words) the basic unit of communication. Speaking of Samuel Beckett's *Waiting for Godot* (1953), for example, he calls it wonderful simply on the level of sound (Stewart 306). Perhaps a parallel project motivates his interest in discrete body parts as units of identity or as legitimate subjects of study in his phenomenological quest to know the world. Maybe he sees them as elements employed to connect with others. His paintings as well, when recognizably naturalistic at all, put forth similar signifiers of the self. In his striking multimedia *Self-Portrait* (2004), a sort of dragon drapes over his forehead, like a hood of bone, like a costume, like a verbal collocation, mediating the space between self and the world (figure 2).

The barest smudges read "man" in context, and the body below the face is rendered in little more than a shoulder's outline echoing the wood-base contour, and an armpit shadow. As in the poems, the medium, here paint and wood rather than sound or language, has been foregrounded, so the surface itself seems tangible, touchable, rather than transparent as in a work of higher realism. Again, the artist has strictly limited himself to a few key details, eyes, lips, in order to tease out potential meanings held somewhere between the image itself and the viewer's effort to understand it.

The way the poetic voice seems to lift out and handle particular words as objects of playful study begins in the book's title *re: f (gesture)* with the implied F-word, *fuck*. The title deconstructs divisions between verbal, visual, and gestural signification by inviting an initial merging of word and body, evoking the physical gesture of the raised middle finger. The word *fuck* suggests many possibilities: a word for the gentlest intersection between two people, a word of anti-romance, a word of violence and transgression, a word threaded through certain discourse communities, rendering them subversive or defiant of hegemonically instated moral norms and values. Everett plays with the power of this word in *Erasure* (2001), in which his provocative protagonist Monk Ellison insists on re-titling his runaway best-seller simply *Fuck*, once the public has shamelessly embraced its racist contents. The poet would probably argue that, like other symbols that become mainstream, this word's force has been diminished through common usage (Stewart 312). According to the function of the parentheses around *gesture*, the said act transpires both within and without the fictive space.[6]

The trajectory of the *(Body)* section of the book, with its two distinct characters and biology textbook renderings, creates a narrative of bodies under scrutiny, bodies in combination. Within the poems, the dynamic drama of the flicking tongue or the squeezing eyelid complement deeper questions of union between body and world through sensual perception

Figure 2. "Self Portrait" by Percival Everett. Credit: *Self-Portrait,* by Percival Everett, Oil on wood, 30" x 36", Collection of Chris Abani, Reproduced by Permission of Percival Everett.

and the rational interpretation of empirical data. As a whole, the poems tell a story of discovering the human body via vision, touch, smell, sound, and the very act of naming, often with labels unfamiliar in their Latin precision. Ironically, the more explicitly specific the word, the more recondite the image is for the lay reader. So, in part, the text tells a tale of deciphering, a metaphoric journey through language that takes place only when the reader enters in. The narrative evolves in the heterosexual union between male and female, anticipated, remembered, or evoked outright in representations: the body; my body (male); her body; your body. Everett would likely call this sequence as plot-driven as *Waiting for Godot,* in that suspense can exist in the reader as s/he attends the next revelation or anticipates: *what thought happens next?*

A question arises, particularly in the blazon tradition, as to whether Everett's bodies are universalized or individualized. The poet employs no names, makes no attempt to describe unique characteristics. The feelings

and urges seem typically human, yet not clichéd, due to the defamiliar-
ized way they are depicted and the aesthetic level the poet achieves. The
erotic arch of the section tapers off finally, to end with the most mundane
yet strangely beautiful activities of breathing, digestion, and blood flow.
Presented as case studies, with their regularized form, their textbook diction, their words carefully chosen and placed, these poems could seem
cold and flat. The tone of fascination sustained throughout creates a sense
of intimacy and empathy instead, and invokes an affective response in the
attentive reader.

Everett's prose and poetry are both central to the contemporary African
American literary canon, and works that pointedly resist racial marking.
The troubled society Everett parodies in his highly acclaimed novel *Erasure* (2001) comes under attack in more subtle, no less powerful ways in
(Body). Here are poems that speak the body and the personal connection
such bodies enable. They trust the perceptions for gaining knowledge in
the human thirst to sensually experience the phenomenal world. The performative act of Everett's observation affirms bodily existence (now under
extremist attack in the digital/new media age), memorializes human inter-
connection, and on a political plane, asserts ownership and self-definition.
Clearly, the poems are written against the artificial ethnic classifications
Everett abhors.[7] Even the sole mention of "pigment," our most deceptive
and clichéd racial marker, suggests nothing of a categorical distinction
between ethnicities ("Labia Majora" 60). The more interesting question
seems to be whether the two bodies depicted throughout the collection
represent specific individuals or simply subject positions somehow relatively safe from the ravages of culture.

However carefully Everett as an artist eschews artificial categories of
ethnicity, in light of his African American ethnicity, this group of nineteen poems, one could argue, extends the tradition of verse celebrating
the African American body as a symbol of self-determination and self-
reliance, and as an expression of the culturally constructed self. Robert
Hayden's "The Tattooed Man" and Yusef Komunyakaa's "Anodyne" com-
pare well as richly voiced poems of the body as expression of the self.[8]
Hayden creates an extended *ecce homo* cry in which the subject displays
an image of Christ's *Last Supper* on his chest, evoking a veritable totem of
western Christian civilization. Komunyakaa's poem, closer to Everett's in

terms of carnal focus, nevertheless references western civilization's reach as well, with the mention of Pan, West Africa, and ragtime rhythms. Everett's *(Body)* poems, however, resist the ethnic-specific and cultural marking of Hayden's and Komunyakaa's poems, by seeking refuge in biology and focusing strictly on the body itself. Everett claims with characteristic exasperation, "I don't want to talk about race. I just want to make art" (Monaghan A18). His aestheticized body parts present themselves as autonomous objects, freed as far as possible from social constructions or identity politics. Indeed, he evokes nature and technology in "Palmar Fascia," using the metaphor of a spreading tree for the muscled hand, with the fingers as satellites. Yet, the carefully selected rhetorical comparisons remain fairly neutral and generalized.

The delicacy and force with which Everett evokes sensual experience recalls, at times, the aesthetics of Jean Toomer's *Cane* (1921).[9] The dynamic descending/ascending tension discussed above ("Obiturator Internus" 49) echoes a passage from *Cane*'s "Box Seat:"

Me, horizontally above her.
Action: perfect strokes downward oblique
Hence, man dominates because of limitation.
Or, so it shall be until women learn their stuff. (124)

Here, unnamed, unspecified bodies interact, and the poetic voice achieves fine precision. Grander philosophies creep in, undercut without drama, expressed in an unpretentious vernacular. As in Everett's poems, the reader often seems to position him/herself at the shoulder of the narrative/poetic voice, sharing in the perceptual experience.

Keith Mitchell has suggested additional blazon examples from the African American literary canon, including Toomer's "Portrait in Georgia" and James Weldon Johnson's "The White Witch." Unlike these poems, however, Everett's *(Body)* poems resist mention of race and often do not differentiate between male and female body parts. Instead of the traditional blazon, in which the male voice deconstructs the female body, Everett's poems include both male and female as subjects of study, as objects of desire for knowledge. Yet, the first four lines of "Portrait in Georgia" (50) could likewise describe either a male or a female subject. However, Everett rarely gestures toward illusory referents, as in Toomer's highly metaphoric "Her Lips are Copper Wire" (101). Nevertheless, both poets collage sense impressions with intense, fragmented imagery. The disorienting switch from one point of view to another—"her words" / "your lips"—also relates to Everett's disorienting technique, imperfectly labeled literary cubism.

Everett renders the female body as well. His unabashed poem "Labia Majora" recalls Rita Dove's ease with the female body in "After Reading *Mickey in the Night Kitchen* for the Third Time Before Bed." Both poets defy social taboos against depicting female genitalia. Yet, Everett's poems have nothing of Dove's autobiographical grounding. Still, the poems seem not to suffer the typical power imbalance when the male gaze confronts a female object, due to the poem's orientation toward empathetic intersubjectivity. The poet also inverts the paradigm of male domination by emphasizing feminine agency in surprising ways: her scent penetrates him though *nasal fossae*, "brushing my bone" (51). The eroticism of this line further empowers the active female. Everett mediates the fictional other's voice as well, such that it may occasionally be either male or female, as an object of desire. Within context, the poems seem to imply a heterosexual coupling, yet often the bodies appear ambiguous—ungendered.

Arguably, the sense of humor that comes through so strongly in Everett's novels surfaces in *re: f (gesture)* in the guise of a more meditative wittiness. Referring to the *sclera* or tough, whitish outer layer of the eyeball, he writes "Sclerotic" in which the poetic voice harmonizes "my eyes" with "your sight, / your vision" (52) creating a balance between seeing and being seen.[10] The see-saw between contrasting perspectives clearly drawn to one another, and the measured pacing of the lines, create a sense of balance. A near obsession with surface, contact, and penetration lends a certain eroticism.

Everett's intimate and confessional tone tempers any sense of dominion, as his eye travels these bodyscapes like a hand moving down the contours of an autonomous figure. By the collection's end, Everett's forms under contemplation coalesce into an integrated whole, not a body, but a text, a book in the reader's hand: a corpus. Defamiliarizing signifying practices that draw attention to the medium of language (or paint) allows for new experiences of the body as idea and as physical reality. Readers can identify with both the poetic voice in the act of perception and with the embodied object perceived. Achieving this intersubjective connection, Everett lifts the corporeal object as far as possible from the weight of cultural norms and values. We come to appreciate the body anew for its forms, its performance, and its facilitation of connections between us. The poet reopens our eyes to the human figure,[11] thereby refreshing our experience of the world that contextualizes it. His linguistic ventures into the warm and responsive body become philosophical investigations into the human attempt to both communicate authentically and to understand.

Notes

1. This term and practice come from Viktor Shklovsky's Russian Formalist theory of estrangement, "Art as Technique" (1917). As a student and teacher of Structuralist Theory, Everett knows these ideas well. Shklovsky's project includes a social welfare platform based on the belief that the renewal of perceptual experience will result in a fuller life for all citizens.

2. Roland Barthes (often a figure in Everett's fiction) creates a distinction in his own *S/Z* between *readerly* and *writerly* texts in his study of Balzac's story "Sarrasine." Frank Lentriccia and Thomas McLaughlin explain, "*Readerly* texts, according to Barthes, 'are products (and not productions)' (Barthes 5). They represent 'a kind of idleness' in which the reader becomes 'intransitive,' a passive receiver. The goal of the *writerly* text, on the other hand, 'is to make the reader no longer a consumer, but a producer of the text'" (Barthes 4). For further discussion, see Barthes, "From Work to Text" (1971).

3. The Everettean fragment requires some caution however. Consider *Glyph*'s (1999) protagonist Ralph's take on such bits: "To call any portion of any language or life or story a fragment is to miss the point or at least beg the question. In fact, there are no fragments, but each part of language, life, or story are, in the spirit of Leibniz's monads, whole, complete, and self-contained. There is no more space between what we routinely and naively refer to as a fragment and its presumed parent whole than there is between me and my name" (184).

4. Consider Ralph's musings on language, using the figure of a wall to specify the freedom and restraint involved in language: "If language was my prison house, then writing was the wall over which I climbed for escape. But climbing the wall either way meant, finally, the same thing, and so language was the prison and the escape and therefore no prison at all, any more than freedom is confinement simply because it precludes one from being confined. Indeed, my much regarded and

remarkable relationship and facility with language had caused my incarceration, but also it had freed me" (*Glyph* 145).

5. Everett's faith in an intersubjective approach seems corroborated by his consistent attention to the individual subjectivity of his characters. Keith Mitchell has traced the title of Everett's second book of poetry *Abstraktion und Einfühlung* (2008) to Husserl student Edith Stein's 1917 doctoral dissertation, "On the Problem of Empathy" ("Zum Problem der Einfühlung") (Conversation 9/09).

6. For more on the question of *fictive space*, see Everett's hilarious satire of Ludwig Wittgenstein's *Tractatus* in *Glyph* (196–97).

7. The poet tells Anthony Stewart, "I can't represent African Americans. No one can . . . . I don't pretend to represent anyone but myself" (303).

8. For a discussion of representations of the African American man in contemporary art, see Thelma Golden, *Black Male: Representations of Masculinity in Contemporary American Art* (New York: Whitney Museum of American Art / H. N. Abrams, 1994). Everett and Komunyakaa have been paired fairly often in recent criticism. See, for example, William M. Ramsey, "Knowing Their Place: Three Black Writers and the Postmodern South," *Southern Literary Journal* 37, no. 2 (Spring 2005): 119–39.

9. Everett frequently alludes to Toomer's touchstone of African American literature *Cane*. Examples include his character Sue Kabnis in *Zulus* (1989) and the conversation between Thelonious and Lisa Ellison in *Erasure* (2001) (Mitchell 8/09).

10. As Ralph reports, "there is no situation more self-affirming as seeing I to I with oneself" (*Glyph* 181).

11. Everett calls for a more attentive readership in "Signing to the Blind," an article whose polemic recalls obliquely Zora Neale Hurston's 1950 essay "What White Publishers Won't Print." Yet, Everett shifts the responsibility of communicating art's truth somewhat from the publishing corporations to the reading public itself, as he did in *Erasure* as well.

Chapter 9

When the Text Becomes the Stage

Percival Everett's Performance Turn in For Her Dark Skin

ROBIN G. VANDER

In the pantheon of Greek tragedies, Euripides's *Medea* stands as a preeminent rendering of desire, scorn, and revenge and continues to enthrall writers, audiences, and academics alike as witnessed through the periodic reinterpretations, translations, and updated performances. With *For Her Dark Skin* (1990), Percival Everett joins the ranks of scholars and authors having attempted a reenvisioning of the work while simultaneously setting himself apart due to his unique envisioning of the text. As a literary novel, the elements traditionally found in a dramatic work—list of characters, stage directions, labeling of scenes and acts—are absent. Nonetheless, despite the shift in literary genres, Everett's rendition acknowledges its origins by creating a text that enlists a performance paradigm as part of its narrative convention. Using an economy of language and sans dramatic setting, Everett's approach to the story of Jason and Medea is constituted in the novel through the collection of intradiegetic narratives serving as the "cast of characters" found in a traditional dramatic work. Through polyphony, parody, and intertextuality, Everett's *For Her Dark Skin* reflects the theoretical turn that renders the text as the stage as writing becomes performance.

The Beginnings of the Text

Performance Studies scholar Dwight Conquergood described performance as that of mimesis—poesis—kinesis whereby a breaking through

139

to experience occurs. In his assessment, Conquergood viewed the ends of performance to be that of dynamic experience rather than the mere creation of a static product and the depth of possibility within performance rests not solely in a final product but rather in the *process*, the experience and consciousness of *doing*; the presence of the intellectual and physical self, the sensory awareness of one's engagement and that of the Other. For Conquergood, the experience within performance evolved as "imitation, construction, dynamism" ("Beyond" 31–32), so that the performing individual moved from mere mimicry, to that of creation and development, and ultimately to the realization of experience *as energy and matter*. Appropriating Conquergood, the intent here is to consider the construction of *For Her Dark Skin* as a "processual movement," extending beyond a repetitious or reverential retelling of Euripides's *Medea* to that of Everett's own breaking through, by means of referential parody and intertextuality, to a meaning making text reimagining narrative itself.

As a novel, *For Her Dark Skin* displaces any notions of adherence to dramatic conventions or to drama as the singular or primary literary genre in which *Medea* can be told. As a parodic text, the novel is simultaneously transgressive and transformative, with the shifting of genres being read as interrogating the historical place drama, and the literary canon itself, have sustained in both cultural productions and the transmission of ideas/ideals and information.[1] If shifting genres in the retelling of *Medea* is regarded as a critique of tradition, categorization, and the canon, then Everett's text begins as an interrogation and a performance. Within the critique of literature's primacy, Nathan Stucky argues:

> Literature is not so much a product for consumption as it is a way of valuing . . . How do we determine, judge, value, and protest the canon? Revisions of "great books" and writers can take place from within and without . . . Part of our contemporary reluctance to speak authoritatively derives from our recognition that literature, rather than standing alone, occupies the same space as other discourse. ("Re/locating the Text" np)

In Everett, this shift destabilizes and contests the primacy of the dramatic narrative and its concretization in the literary canon; as such, the novel slowly materializes as that of a performance text reinvisioning literature as discourse and reformulating the response to the question, "Who speaks?" If performance is about the interaction between speaking subjects, then what follows is a structuralist argument for viewing the performance text/performative writing as reflecting similar interaction between texts by virtue of the intertextual nature of Everett's narrative. With regards to genre crossing, there is a consideration to be made as to how new opportunities for analysis and artistic imagining arise when the narrative is extricated from a single literary genre. This multiplicity of genres contributes to what Conquergood had regarded as a destabilization. Viewing this blurring of artistic productions as a political act, there arises in the interstitial spaces of those productions the "commingling of analytical and artistic way of knowing that unsettles the institutional organization of knowledge and discipline" ("Performance Studies" 151). Noting Everett's refusal to be categorized, the idea of "blurring, comingling, and unsettling" appears apropos to any assessments that might be made of Everett's novel or of his other works.[2] The visual appearance of *For Her Dark Skin*, the printed page, creates a "co-text" to that of the original performed text. Its nontheatrical qualities clearly establish differences from its dramatic origins and despite the technological reproducibility and the notationality of the text, the narrative and its construction are parodic reminders of the inability to set Everett or his work in one light or another. The marked differences between *For Her Dark Skin* and *Medea* become apparent given that the "the non-reproducibility of theatrical performance depends on the ephemeral and transitory quality of its presence" (De Marinis 237). Thus the novel becomes the story of Jason and Medea yet in its difference reminds readers that it is also not the play. While the narrative is constituted by performance it is not a performance text. The juxtaposition of what the novel is/is not reflects its own possibilities within the realm of the potential for performance in/as narrative.[3]

That Everett is a prolific writer and literary scholar cannot be overlooked in an understanding of his creative works. Given his own entrenchment in literary theory, Everett's genre blurring cannot only be regarded as a performance but can also be read as an act of signifying. In the essay "Performing Writing," Della Pollock speaks of writing as a metonymic performance and states, "Metonymic writing invokes the presence of what it isn't ironically, by elaborating what it is—by either camping on its own forms or running them to the limit or hyperbolizing the symbol-signifier as the figment of print and punctuation" ("Performing Writing" 85). In its slim 152 pages, *For Her Dark Skin*, written not in scenes and acts but rather in a series of eight chapters comprised of character narratives each consisting of no more than two pages in length becomes a parodic text of not only Greek tragedy but also of the idea of the novel as genre. It exists as a novel/idea continuously calling into presence and questioning, an absence. *For Her Dark Skin* reminds the reader/audience that it is not the dramatic work *Medea*, yet it engenders our reflecting on that work and its erasure/interpretation in Everett's hands. The novel becomes a literary embodiment of Everett at work/play. As a parodic text, it is illustrative of the "stylizations" described in M. M. Bakhtin's theories of the novel and narrative discourse as occupying "an essential place in the novel" including its irony, humor, elements of self-parody . . . and the insertion of indeterminancy" rendering "a certain semantic openendedness" (6–7).

Narratives. Bodies. Race.

As a novel, the text is constructed as a dialogic narrative constituted by the reflections of Jason, Medea, the Nurse, Tamar, and Polydeuces; no one character's worldview holds supremacy over the others. Through intersecting narratives, the novel develops a panoramic view of Greek culture and society, race, relationships, and trauma. Each character provides an integral element to the novel's development, and the multiplicity and diversity of voices in the novel establish a heteroglossia simultaneously reflecting the unity and disunity of speaking subjects within fictive communities. Given the various narratives within the novel, *For Her Dark Skin* becomes a social text, one of social relations, incapable of being collapsed into one unified monologic position. Instead, the novel becomes illustrative of the "Bakhtinian novel"—one of dialogic interaction, polyphonous or multivoiced—where each chapter/character serves as narrator, neither subordinated to the other. For Bakhtin, thus in Everett, "Dialogue here is not the threshold to action, it is the action itself . . . To be means to communicate dialogically. When dialogue ends, everything ends" (Bakhtin, *Problems of Dostoevsky's Poetics* 252). The novel's reimagining of *Medea* produces a discourse heightened by race and cultural differences witnessed at the outset of the narrative in the first line spoken by Jason, "To a land of darker-skinned people" described as "too uncooperative and too large" to row a ship. Continuing to reflect on race and characteristics he states, "A dark man from that land might not pull an oar at all, but stare at you blankly as if there were something to be understood. You could flog the poor bastard senseless and still he would leave you the worse, wondering what it was you had failed to see" (6). Though Jason's first words in the novel focus on the black men of Colchis, most reflections in the novel will focus on Medea, rendering a raced and sexed reading of her body by virtually all other characters. For her part, Medea's narrative is interspersed with pejorative thoughts toward Jason, in particular, reflecting on his fair complexion and that only a spell cast by some unnamed god could have made her love someone of his appearance and stature. She states, "He was not much to look at and really not much for anything else. Seeing him strut around as he did, I expected the son of a god, but all I got was a pale man just off a boat . . . I would not have let him touch me, but the gods . . . not even my gods, but some chalked-skinned, bitch voyeur caused me to fall in love with this Jason" (10).

From the opening lines to the novel's fiery ending, the racialized discourse emanates from the social context in which each character has been situated, to such an extent, as to have both Jason and Medea subjectively inscribe their infant sons' bodies with racial identification. For her, "My babies. They were so beautiful . . . I believed them to carry my magic. Their skin shone only a bit of my pigment, but enough to mark their distinction from the pale populace" (112). For him, "Such strong and handsome boys. Hung like bulls. With hair the color of the morning sun. They looked so much alike" (114). While both Jason and Medea choose only to see themselves and not each other in their sons' appearances, they reject the existence of the other in the corporeal reality of the infants' bodies. Each parent's attempt to erase the presence of the other by solely noting his/her own self reflected in the physical appearance of each baby, in actuality highlights the absence of the other. As performance, the erasure inadvertently—parodically—calls into existence that of the Other. Within performance, the tenets of embodiment and copresence are pivotal in meaning making due to the importance of engagement. Thus, Everett's fictive depiction of this erasure structurally reconnects readers to how race has been referenced throughout the course of the narrative. These references are no less performances that reflect awareness, engagement, and deliberate erasure of the Other and are thus read as charged with "intention and direction towards an object" (Bakhtin, *Discourse in the Novel* 276–77); in this instance, character depictions of explicit awareness of different and racialized backgrounds.

Through a performance lens, an examination as to how Everett acknowledges race in the narrative allows for a Bakhtinian analysis of character depictions and considerations of the various forms of narration within the text, including those that reveal characters as speaking subjects both historically and socially situated. In her assessment of differing narrative constructions between drama and the novel, Pollock enlists Bakhtin's concepts of the novel that have relevance for this discussion of Everett. She states:

> In its most authentic, "double-voiced" form, then, language may subvert its own constructions. The language of the Bakhtinian novel is mercurial . . . But even insofar as it is a medium of interaction, language is also context-bound; it is "ideologically saturated" and ideologically empowered . . . In other words, language is, at any given moment, double-voiced: it does not deny its interactive identity by gravitating toward "a single consciousness or a single voice" but intrinsically echoes the speech contexts, generations, and social collectives between which it passes . . . language is in itself neither neutral nor abstractly normative. It is, rather, "a concrete heteroglot conception of the world." ("The Play as Novel" 298)

Performance, as a discipline predicated on embodied ways of knowing, engages the Others' speaking body revealing it as a sentient medium and product of research that, according to Paul Connerton, can be situated as a repository of "past events." Through descriptions of gestures, postures, movements, and positionality, it is mnemonic and enacts performative utterances revealing historical and cultural influences, allowing for the study of "voice" and "body" as agents of rhetorical performances. Connerton suggests these practices are "traces" of history and reflecting "social memory" (13).

Theory as Performance

Through the lens of performance, the text of *For Her Dark Skin* creates a narrative illustrative of the theoretical concept of performativity and what can be perceived to be its enlistment by Everett in constructing Euripides in the novel. Building on Elin Diamond's clarification of performativity based upon Austin's concept of the linguistic utterance, the narrative becomes a measure of citationality. According to Diamond, "Performativity derives from J. L. Austin's concept of the performative utterance which does not refer to an extra-linguistic reality but rather enacts or produces that to which it refers" (4). In what is deemed performative, a prior utterance or act is called into being, into existence through contemporary practices and acts of embodiment. Twice in the novel, Euripides as author is referenced. First, in the fourth chapter entitled "Corinth," Tamar introduces readers to the existence of Euripides as she listens to the predicament Medea considers herself to be in in loving Jason. Acknowledging that her feelings are the result of darts sent by Eros, Medea states, "So I am in love with a man whom I despise. The thought of his inadequate tool dipping into the life-well of my body sickens me. But I must have it" (81). To which Tamar thinks to herself, "What does one say? I just sat there, stunned by such revelations. I would write to my cousin Euripides; he would appreciate this story" (81). Interpreting this exchange between Medea and Tamar, this passage is read as performance bringing Everett's reader into contact with the future writer Euripides, who will become the literary progenitor for Everett and his novel, *For Her Dark Skin*. In this early introduction to Euripides, readers encounter him *not* as the author of *Medea*, the original text, but as cousin to Tamar and *prospective* author of *a text*. In the sixth chapter "The Leaving," Tamar pens a letter to Euripides, "Rip," updating him of the events occurring in Corinth:

3 Thasos Court

Corinth

Euripides

7 Heracles Lane

Athens

Dear Rip,

Much has happened since I last wrote to you. Medea gave birth . . . I was present at the delivery. It was very noisy as one might expect . . . You should be here witnessing this mess. Jason has become more involved with King Creon's child-daughter and rumor has it that—well, you can guess . . . Where this leaves Medea, I do not know . . . Polydeuces is fine. He sends his best and says he looks forward to meeting you. He wishes you good luck with your writing . . .

Love,

Tamar (Everett 100–111)

The parody found in *For Her Dark Skin* materializes as metanarrative—metaperformance, if you will—in recognizing Everett's fictionalizing the eventuality of Euripides someday writing *Medea*. Through performativity and parody, Everett calls into being Euripides, not solely as character within the novel but ultimately as the author of the iconic Greek tragedy *Medea* of which the novel, *For Her Dark Skin*, finds its inspiration. The letter to Cousin "Rip" serves as the site and citation of Euripides and *Medea*, Everett and the novel, conjoined, becoming the embodiment of authors and texts—plural. The performance turn within the narrative sets the text as stage for Everett's calling into being his own existence: Euripides as emerging writer is read as *someday* authoring *Medea*, the dramatic work that will inspire generations of authors and texts including Everett and the novel, *For Her Dark Skin*. Through Tamar's suggestion of writing to "Rip," the performative element of the letter now calls into being the original text *Medea* in its nascent stage. The letter alone represents a deeply theoretical moment in the construction of the narrative: from the perspective of performance it is the fictive embodiment of literary authors and texts, through structuralism the narrative illustrates the connection to all other narratives emanating from *Medea*. And still, through a Russian Formalist reading one can solely assess the literary conventions on the page for their efficacy in rendering an engaging and intelligible narrative external to any other critical perspectives or contexts. Again citing Pollock, "Performative writing is evocative. It operates metaphorically to render absence present . . . It does not describe, in a narrowly reportorial sense an objectively verifiable event or process but uses language like paint to create what is self-evidently a version of what was, what is, and/or what might be" ("Writing" 80).

Performative, evocative writing evolves in liminal fields heavily fertilized with possibility. Performative writing, consciously moving through Conquergood's paradigm of "mimesis-poesis-kinesis" recovers presence rendering it visible in a non-mimetic, non-static manner. Because Tamar's wondering of whether or not the events would make a good story that her cousin would write about we, the readers, are given a fictionalized and parodic glimpse into "Cousin Rip" on the cusp of becoming the author, Euripides. Through the text, the audience witnesses history and cultural production unfolding on the contemporary literary pages of *For Her Dark Skin* where one text engenders another. *For Her Dark Skin* reinscribes *Medea*, ultimately serving as a fictive self-fulfilling prophecy whereby Euripides and *Medea* inspire Everett and the novel. In this instance, the text is a parodic performance on the construction of narrative, the development of the text and its public reception, and the imitations, parodies, and the reimaginings it will eventually inspire. On this notion of writing as performance and Euripides constructed as a performative utterance in the text, one is reminded of Foucault's seminal essays "What is an Author?" and "What is a Text?," and the relevance structuralism gains in reading Everett, in theorizing that neither the text nor the author are produced or reside in isolation of others that have gone before them. Each, author and text, enters into discursive systems, engaging in dialogic and intertextual exchanges, bearing semblances to articulations that have previously occurred. By invoking Euripides in the novel, Everett performs a meta-genealogy linking *For Her Dark Skin* to its literary ancestor.

Intertexuality as Women Write

Considering Everett's novel, there is another argument for his use of intertextuality in the development of the narrative. Though there are only
two concrete inclusions in the narrative they warrant brief discussion. As
previously stated, in chapter 6 "The Leaving" entails the letter written to
Euripides from Tamar, and in chapter 5, "Giving Birth," a poem written in
Medea's voice is included. Both poem and letter are created on the evening
when Medea gives birth to her twin sons. Prior to the letter, readers will
have encountered Medea's poem:

> I
> will hold them in my body. Watch them,
> feel them
> dissolve,
> Jason, you bastard.
>   But the bastard is not
> here.
> Tamar,
> take my hand,
> squeeze it,
> give me strength to
> hold on.
>   Damn you, Athena.
>   Damn you, Eros.
>   Damn this world.
>   Oh, here they come.
>   There is a
> head.
> There is my baby.
> My soul, my soul.
>   Here is another.
> Breathe, please breathe.
> Oh, Tamar.
>   Oh, my babies.
> Oh, Tamar, my friend. (108)

Written in free verse, the poem serves as a summary of the chapter; Medea's attempts to dissolve her unborn children in her belly, Jason's abandonment, the curse of and cursing the work of Eros, birthing twins, and her budding friendship with Tamar. Both the poem and the letter, respectively, constitute the "narrating instance" predicated on each character's subjectivity in the novel. Tamar's letter reiterates events in Corinth from her point of view, while Medea's poem is a recitation of recent events and her experiences. In both the letter and the poem, a close reading of the texts locates a "dialogic site-ing"/citing of early narrative forms predating the existence of the novel: the epistle and the poetic verse. That the only characters in the novel granted self-expression through writing are females lends itself possibly to a feminist reading of the narrative and the questioning of Everett's performance of granting authorial privilege to women. The letter and the poem become emancipatory acts imagining women's lived experiences that signify on the currency of expressive culture. In particular, Tamar's letter cites the primacy given writing as a performance of self-actualization and scrutiny, and elevates the character to that of an observer and witness at the scene of knowledge production. Both Tamar and Medea subvert hierarchical claims of authorship and interrogate the age-old question, "Who speaks/who writes?"

Everett's inclusion of the poem and the letter suggests the entanglements of literary conventions that go into the production of any text. As performance, the poem and the letter remind readers that embedded within the narrative, embedded within the novel we discover those earlier utterances predating prose fiction, utterances bisecting time and genre. Dwelling within the novel is the multiplicity of texts—poem, epistle, drama—folding one into the other, transgressing and intersecting genres, giving form to fiction. In this genealogy of narratives, the utterances move from constative, words reporting what other words and people do, to that of performative whereby words that do what other words report. The poem and the letter are performances of citationality requiring no quotation marks. The discursive community already grasps their meanings and signification.

Writing as performance is always an act of self-actualization, destabilization, citationality, and openendedness. Always already situated in the production of the text is an awareness of an absence being rendered visible as the narrative evolves. The simultaneity of an evolving narrative—unfolding, enfolding prior texts and utterances—fosters the conjoined seriousness and playfulness that we find in creative and critical writing. The writing becomes a performance of processual activity that moves in the direction of breaking through to meaning.

As an author, Everett continuously signifies on literary productions, reinscribing texts and authors with new meanings and interpretations. By means of performance, his writing becomes evocative, often calling himself and others into being in the text. In *For Her Dark Skin* writing can be seen as a reflection of literary and genre studies where the text becomes the stage and narrative renders visible not simply characters and worlds of the author's creation, but renders visible the author himself.

Notes

1. Tangentially, the shift from drama to novel invokes a consideration of the roles drama and theater have played in society. Here, Augusto Boal's *Theatre of the Oppressed* comes to mind, in particular, the scholar's argument of the function of theater to transmit messages to audiences that sought to educate and to instruct about social norms and ideologies. Boal suggested that theater as a medium of communication was enlisted by church, state, and nobility as a means of disseminating messages that ultimately reinforced the status quo and existing hierarchies. In noting control of the theater, he noted control of the message and thus the populace. To subvert and change the structure, it was thus incumbent upon the lower statused to gain access to the medium and disseminate new messages that encouraged rethinking and restructuring society. Invoking Boal to consider Everett, my interest is situated in rethinking Everett's collective body of work as an ongoing exercise in destabilization. Here, *For Her Dark Skin* as a novel calls into examination genre studies, the literary canon, and academic discourse that would reiterate if not concretize the story of Jason and Medea in its original dramatic form.

2. Here as elsewhere throughout *Perspectives on Percival Everett*, several are indebted to Anthony Stewart's "Uncategorizable Is Still a Category: An Interview With Percival Everett" for its presentation of Everett in his own words and his rejection of concrete definitions applied to himself as a writer or to his work. My considerations of genre blurring are an acknowledgment of that sentiment and how it is continuously reflected throughout Everett's work.

3. As a performance text, I am regarding the novel in what D. Soyini Madison terms "the politics of possibility"; that is, the text becomes a means for interrogating existing worlds. In this case, the literary genre and social discourse. While Madison discusses "the politics of possibility" within the context of performance ethnography and more along the lines of interpretive social science studies, the concept is applicable here to considering how cultural productions, including dramatic works and the literary texts, serve as means of engaging other voices and experiences, and the world of the Other. The opening of one's self to engaging those voices, experiences, and worlds is writ large in the possibility for a burgeoning understanding and empathy toward others/the Other.

Works Cited

Appiah, Kwame Anthony. *Cosmopolitanism: Ethics in a World of Strangers*. Issues of Our Times Series. Series edited by Henry Louis Gates Jr. New York: Norton, 2006. Print.

Baird, Lisa. "A Churning in My Gut." *Thinking Black: Some of the Nation's Best Black Columnists Speak Their Minds*. Edited by DeWayne Wichkam. New York: Crown, 1996. 160–62. Print.

Baker, Houston. *Blues, Ideology, and Afro-American Literature: A Vernacular Theory*. Chicago: University of Chicago Press, 1984. Print.

Bakhtin, M. M. *The Dialogic Imagination. Four Essays*. Translated by Caryl Emerson and Michael Holquist. Edited by Michael Holquist. Austin: University of Texas Press, 1990. Print.

——. *Problems of Dostoevsky's Poetics*. Edited and translated by Caryl Emerson. *Theory and History of Literature*, vol. 8. Edited by Wlad Godzich and Jochen Schulte-Sasse. Minneapolis: University of Minneapolis Press, 1984. Print.

Barthes, Roland. "From Work to Text" (1971). *Textual Strategies*. Edited by Josue V. Harari. Ithaca, NY: Cornell University Press, 1979. Print.

——. *S/Z*. Translated by Richard Miller. London: Jonathan Cape, 1974. Print.

——. *The Rustle of Language*. Translated by Richard Howard. Berkeley and Los Angeles: University of California Press, 1989. Print.

Beatty, Paul. *White Boy Shuffle*. New York: Picador, 1996. Print.

Bell, Bernard W. *The Afro-American Novel and Its Tradition*. Amherst: University of Massachusetts Press, 1987. Print.

Benhabib, Seyla. *Another Cosmopolitanism*. The Berkeley Tanner Lectures. Edited by Robert Post. Oxford: Oxford University Press, 2006. Print.

Berben-Masi, Jacqueline. "Percival Everett's *Glyph*: Prisons of the Body, Physical, Political, and Academic." *In the Grip of the Law: Trials, Prisons, and the Space Between*. Edited by Monka Fludernik and Greta Olson. Frankfurt: Peter Lang, 2004. 223–39. Print.

Bhabha, Homi K. *The Location of Culture*. New York: Routledge, 1994. Print.

Bishop, Norma. "A Nigerian Version of a Greek Classic: Soyinka's Transformation of *The Bacchae*." *Research in African Literatures* 14, no. 1, Special Issue on Wole Soyinka (Spring 1983): 68–80.

Brandon, George. *Santeria from Africa to the New World: The Dead Sell Memories*. Bloomington: Indiana University Press, 1993.

Burke, Kenneth. *A Rhetoric of Motives*. Berkeley and Los Angeles: University of California Press, 1969.

Cassuto, Leonard. *The Inhuman Race: The Racial Grotesque in American Literature and Culture*. New York: Columbia University Press, 1997. Print.

Connerton, Paul. *How Societies Remember*. Themes in the Social Sciences. Cambridge: Cambridge University Press, 1989; rpt., 1995.

Conquergood, Dwight. "Beyond the Text: Toward a Performative Cultural Politics." *The Future of Performance Studies: Visions and Revisions*. Edited by S. J. Dailey. Washington, DC: National Communication Association, 1998. 25–36. Print.

———. "Performance Studies: Interventions and Radical Research." *Drama Review* 46, no. 2 (2002): 145–56.

Danquah, Meri Nana-Ama. *The Black Body*. New York: Seven Stories Press, 2009. Print.

De Marinis, Marco. "The Performance Text." *The Performance Studies Reader*. Edited by Henry Bial. London: Routledge, 2004. Print.

Descartes, Rene. *Discourse on Method and Meditations on First Philosophy*. Translated by Donald Cress. 4th ed.Indianapolis: Hackett, 1998. Print.

Deutsch, James I. "The Bad Man." *The Greenwood Encyclopedia of African American Folklore*. Edited by Anand Prahlad. Westport, CT: Greenwood Press, 2006. Print.

Diamond, Elin. "Introduction." *Performance and Cultural Politics*. London: Routledge, 1996. Print.

Du Bois, W. E. B. *Black Reconstruction in America: 1860–1880*. New York: Free Press, 1935/1999.

Douglass, Frederick. *My Bondage and My Freedom*. Urbana: University of Illinois Press, 1987.

Dove, Rita. "After Reading *Mickey in the Night Kitchen* for the Third Time Before Bed." *Grace Notes*. New York: Norton, 1989. 41. Print.

Duncan, Bowie. "Jean Toomer's *Cane*: A Modern Black Oracle." *College Language Association Journal* 15, no. 3 (March 1972): 323–33.

Eaton, Kimberly. "Race Under Erasure." *Callaloo* 28, no. 2 (2005): 358–68. *JSTOR*. http://www.jstor.org/stable/3805659. Online.

Eggins, Suzanne. *An Introduction to Systemic Functional Linguistics*. 2nd ed. London: Continuum International Publishing Group, 2007. Print.

Eliade, Mircea. *The Sacred and the Profane: The Nature of Religion.* Translated by Willard R. Trask. New York: Harvest, 1968. Print.

Ellis, Trey. "The New Black Aesthetic." *Callaloo* 38 (Winter 1989): 233–43. Print.

Ellison, Ralph. *Flying Home and Other Stories.* New York: Random House, 1996.

——. "Flying Home." *Flying Home and Other Stories.* Edited by John F. Callahan. 147–73.

——. *Invisible Man.* 2nd ed. New York: Vintage, 1995. Print.

——. *Shadow and Act.* 1953. New York: Vintage, 1995. Print.

Everett, Percival. *Abstraktion und Einfühlung.* Los Angeles: Black Goat, *2008.*

——. *American Desert.* New York: Hyperion, 2004. Print.

——. *Cutting Lisa.* Baton Rouge: Louisiana State University Press, 2000. Print.

——. *Erasure.* St. Paul: Hyperion, 2001. Print.

——. *For Her Dark Skin.* Seattle: Owl Creek Press, 1990. Print.

——. *Frenzy.* St. Paul: Graywolf Press, 1997.

——. "Foreword." *Making Callaloo: 25 Years of Black Literature.* Edited by Charles Henry Rowell. New York: St. Martin's Press, 2002. Print.

——. *Glyph.* St. Paul: Graywolf Press, 1999. Print.

——. *I Am Not Sidney Poitier.* St. Paul: Graywolf Press, 2009. Print.

——. *re: f (gesture).* Los Angeles: Black Goat, 2006. Print.

——. "Signing to the Blind." *Callaloo* 14, no. 1 (Winter 1991): 9–11. *JSTOR.* http://www.jstor.org/stable/2931420. Online.

——. *Suder.* Baton Rouge: Louisiana State University Press, 1983. Print.

——. *The Water Cure.* St. Paul: Graywolf Press, 2007. Print.

——. *Zulus.* Sag Harbor: Permanent, 1990. Print.

Fauset, Jessie Redmon. *The Chinaberry Tree: A Novel of American Life.* New York: G. K. Hall and Company, 1931/1995.

Foucault, Michel. "This Is Not a Pipe." *Aesthetics, Method, and Epistemology.* Edited by James D. Faubion. Translated by Robert Hurley. 3 vols. New York: New Press, 1998. Print.

——. "What Is an Author?" *Aesthetics, Method, and Epistemology.* Edited by James D. Faubion. Translated by Robert Hurley and Others. 3 vols. New York: New Press, 1998. Print.

Golden, Thelma. *Black Male: Representations of Masculinity in Contemporary American Art.* New York: Whitney Museum of American Art / H. N. Abrams, 1994. Print.

Grandt, Jurgen E. "So What?" Introduction. *Kinds of Blue: The Jazz Aesthetics in African American Narrative.* Columbus: Ohio State University Press, 2005. xi–xix. Print.

Grube, George Maximilian Antony. "Dionysus in the *Bacchae.*" *Transactions and Proceedings of the American Philological Association* 66 (1935): 37–54.

Hawkins, Alphonso W. Introduction. *The Jazz Trope: A Theory of African American Literary and Vernacular Culture*. New York: Scarecrow Press, 2008. Print.

Hayden, Robert. "The Tattooed Man." *Collected Poems*. Edited by Frederick Glaysher. New York: Liveright Publishing Corp. 160–62. Print.

Henderson, Carol, ed. *America and the Black Body: Identity Politics in Print and Visual Culture*. Madison: Fairleigh Dickinson University Press, 2009. Print.

Henson, Kristen. *Beyond the Sound Barrier: The Jazz Controversy in Twentieth-Century American Fiction*. New York: Routledge, 2003. 1–10. Print.

Herodotus. *Euterpe* (Book II/Entry 49). London: George Bell and Sons, 1898.

Hogue, W. Lawrence. *The African American Male, Writing, and Difference: A Polycentric Approach to African American Literature, Criticism, and History*. New York: SUNY Press, 2003. Print.

Hughes, Langston. *The Ways of White Folks*. New York: Knopf, 1934. Print.

Hurston, Zora Neale. "What White Publishers Won't Print" (1950). *I Love Myself When I am Laughing . . . And Then Again When I am Looking Mean and Impressive: A Zora Neale Hurston Reader*. Edited by Alice Walker. Old Westbury, NY: Feminist Press, 1979. Print.

"Interview with Sidney Poitier." *CNN Larry King Live*. May 2, 2008. http://transcripts.cnn.com. Online.

Jarrett, Gene Andrew. *African American Literature beyond Race: An Alternative Reader*. New York: New York University Press, 2006.

Johnson, James Weldon. *Autobiography of an Ex-Colored Man*. New York: Sherman, French and the Company/Knopf, 1912/1927. Print.

———. "The White Witch." *The Book of American Negro Poetry*. Edited by James Weldon Johnson. New York: Harcourt, Brace and Company, 1922. Print.

Johnson, Charles. "A Phenomenology of the Black Body." *America and the Black Body: Identity Politics in Print and Visual Culture*. Edited by Carol Henderson. Madison: Fairleigh Dickinson University Press, 2009. 252–65. Print.

Johnson, E. Patrick. *Appropriating Blackness: Performance and the Politics of Authenticity*. Durham, NC: Duke University Press, 2003. Print.

Johnson, Michael L. *Hunger for the Wild: America's Obsession with the Untamed West*. Lawrence: University Press of Kansas, 2007. Print.

Jones, LeRoi. *Blues People: Black Music in White America*. New York: William Morrow, 1963. Print.

Kazin, Alfred. *A Writer's America: Landscape in Literature*. New York: Knopf, 1988. Print.

Keb' Mo'. "Dirty Low Down and Bad." *Keb' Mo'*. New York, 1994. CD.

Kincaid, Jim. "An Interview with Percival Everett." *Callaloo* 28, no. 2 (2005): 377–81. Print.

Kolodny, Annette. *The Lay of the Land: Metaphor as Experience and History in American Life and Letters*. Chapel Hill: University of North Carolina Press, 1975. Print.

Kristeva, Julia. *Powers of Horror: An Essay on Abjection*. New York: Columbia University Press, 1982. Print.

Komunyakaa, Yusef. "Anodyne." *Pleasure Dome: New & Collected Poems*. Middletown, CT: Wesleyan University Press, 2001. Print.

Lacan, Jacques. "The Psychoses 1955–1956." *The Seminar of Jacque Lacan: Book III*. Edited by Jacques-Alain Miller. New York: W. W. Norton, 1993. Print.

Lane, Dermot A. *Foundations for a Social Theology: Praxis, Process and Salvation*. New York: Paulist Press, 1984.

Larsen, Nella. *Quicksand*. New York: Penguin, 1928/2003. Print.

Lentricchia, Frank, and Thomas McLaughlin. *Critical Terms for Literary Study*. 2nd ed. Chicago: University of Chicago Press, 1990. Print.

Levine, Lawrence W. *Black Culture and Consciousness: African American Thought from Slavery to Freedom*. 1977. New York: Oxford University Press, 2007. Print.

Lippi-Green, Rosina. *English with an Accent: Language, Ideology, and Discrimination in the United States*. London: Routledge, 1997. Print.

Marshall, Paule. *Brown Girl, Brownstones*. New York: Feminist Press, 1959/2006. Print.

Martin, Peter J. "Spontaneity and Organization." *The Cambridge Companion to Jazz*. Edited by Mervyn Cook and David Horn. New York: Cambridge University Press, 2002. 133–52. Print.

Marx, Leo. *The Machine in the Garden: Technology and the Pastoral Ideal in America*. New York: Oxford University Press, 1964/2000. Print.

———. *The Pilot and the Passenger: Essays on Literature, Technology, and Culture in the United States*. New York: Oxford University Press, 1988. Print.

Masiki, Trent. "Irony and Ecstasy: A Profile of Percival Everett." *Poets & Writers* (May–June 2004): 33–39. Print.

McKay, Claude. *Home to Harlem*. Lebanon: Northeastern University Press, 1928/1987. Print.

Monaghan, Peter. "Satiric Inferno." *Chronicle of Higher Education*, February 11, 2005: A18+.

Morrison, Toni. *Song of Solomon*. New York: Knopf, 1977. Print.

———. *Jazz*. New York: Knopf, 1992.

Moynihan, Daniel Patrick. *The Negro Family: The Case for National Action*. Washington, D.C.: Office of Policy and Research, U.S. Department of Labor, 1965. Print.

Murray, Albert. *The Hero and the Blues*. New York: Vintage, 1973. Print.

Nicholes, Charles H. "Sterling Brown, Poet, His Place in Afro-American Literary History." *The Harlem Renaissance: Revaluations*. Edited by Amritjit Singh, William S. Shiver, and Stanley Brodwin. New York: Garland Publishing, 1989. 91–100. Print.

Nouryeh, Andrea J. "Soyinka's Euripides: Postcolonial Resistance or Avant-Garde Adaptation?" *Research in African Literatures* 32, no. 4 (Winter 2001): 160–71.

Okpewho, Isidore. "Soyinka, Euripides, and the Anxiety of Empire." *Research in African Literatures* 30, no. 4 Drama and Performance (Winter 1999): 32–55.

Pollock, Della. "The Play as Novel: Reappropriating Brecht's *Drums in the Night*." *Quarterly Journal of Speech* 74 (1988): 296–309.

———. "Performing Writing." *The Ends of Performance*. Edited by Peggy Phelan and Jill Lane. New York: New York University Press, 1998. 73–103. Print.

Ramsey, William R. "Knowing Their Place: Three Black Writers and the Postmodern South." *Southern Literary Journal* 37, no. 2 (Spring 2005): 119–39. Print.

Reed, Ishmael. *Flight to Canada*. New York: Random House, 1976.

Russett, Margaret. "Race Under Erasure." *Callaloo* 28, no. 2 (2005): 358–69. Print.

Sanchez-Arce, Ana Maria. "Authenticism, or the Authority of Authenticity." *Mosaic* 40, no. 3 (September 2007): 139–55. Print.

Scheese, Don. *Nature Writing: The Pastoral Impulse in America*. New York: Routledge, 1995/2002. Print.

Schuller, Gunther. *Early Jazz: Its Roots and Musical Development*. New York: Oxford University Press, 1968. Print.

Schur, Richard. Message to the editor. June 24, 2009. E-mail.

———. "Stomping the Blues No More? Hip Hop Aesthetics and Contemporary African American Literature." *New Essays on the African American Novel: From Hurston to Ellison and Whitehead*. Edited by Lovalerie King and Linda Selzer. New York: Palgrave MacMillan, 2009. 201–21. Print.

Senna, Danzy. *Caucasia*. New York: Riverhead, 1998. Print.

Shklovsky, Viktor. "Art as Technique." *Literary Theory: An Anthology*. Translated by Lee T. Lemon and Marion J. Reis. Edited by Julie Rivkin and Michael Ryan. 2nd ed. Malden: Blackwell Publishing, 2004. 17–21. Print.

———. "Art as Technique." Translated by Lee T. Lemon and Marion J. Reis. *Modern Criticism and Theory: A Reader*. London: Longman, 1988. 16–30. Print.

Smith, Daniel, and John Protevi. "Gilles Deleuze." *Stanford Encyclopedia of Philosophy*. May 23, 2008.http://plato.stanford.edu/entries/deleuze/ (accessed August 26, 2001). Online.

Stewart, Anthony. "Uncategorizable Is Still a Category: An Interview with Percival Everett." *Canadian Review of American Studies* 37, no. 3 (2007): 293–24. Print.

Stucky, Nathan. "Re/locating the Text: Literature in Performance Studies Practice." *Communication Education* 45 (April 1996). (np). Web.

Thoreau, Henry David. *Walden or, Life in the Woods and On the Duty of Civil Disobedience*. New York: Signet Classic, 1854/1960. Print.

Toomer, Jean. *Cane*. New York: Boni and Liveright, 1923/2011. Print.

———. Letter to Waldo Frank. December 12, 1922. JTP 3:6 Beinecke Rare Book and Manuscript Library, Yale University. New Haven. Print.

———. "Portrait in Georgia." *Cane*. Boni and Liveright, 1923/1951. Print.

Tracy, Steven C. "The Blues Novel." *The Cambridge Companion to the African American Novel*. Edited by Maryemma Graham. New York: Cambridge University Press, 2004. 122–38. Print.

Waldron, Jeremy. "What Is Cosmopolitanism?" *Journal of Political Philosophy* 8, no. 2 (2000): 227–43. Print.

We-han Ho, Fred. "What Makes Jazz the Revolutionary Music of the 20th Century, and Will It Be Revolutionary for the 21st Century?" *African American Review* 29, no. 2 (1995): 283–90. Print.

Westling, Louise H. *The Green Breast of the New World: Landscape, Gender, and American Fiction*. Athens: University of Georgia Press, 1995. Print.

White, Joseph L., and James H. Cones III. *Black Man Emerging: Facing the Past and Seizing a Future in America*. New York: Routledge, 1999. Print.

Wyman, Sarah. Message to the editor. September 19, 2009. E-mail.

Contributors

UZZIE CANNON is an Assistant Professor of English at Georgia Gwinnett College where she teaches African American and American literatures. Her research focuses on the intersections of gender, race, and narrative form in contemporary black men's fiction. She has published works in the *African American Review* and the *Southern Literary Journal*. Dr. Cannon is currently exploring the function of the personal journal in contemporary fiction.

JONATHAN DITTMAN is adjunct faculty in the Department of English at the University of St. Thomas in St. Paul, Minnesota. His research interests include African American literature and cultural identity, as well as Dante Aligheri's *Divine Commedia*. He is currently pursuing an M.F.A. in creative writing at Goddard College and is working on a collection of short stories.

RONALD DORRIS holds the Alumni Class of 1958 Professorship in Liberal Arts in African American Studies and English at Xavier University of Louisiana. His research and teaching area is African, African American, and American cultural and intellectual history. He is the author of *Race: Jean Toomer's Swan Song*. His scholarly works appear in *The Forum on Public Policy: A Journal of the Oxford Round Table*, *Proteus*, *McNeese Review*, *Perspectives of Black Popular Culture*, *Black Sacred Music*, *The Griot: Journal of African American Studies*, and *Sparks of Resistance, Flames of Change: Black Communities and Activism*.

FRÉDÉRIC DUMAS is an Assistant Professor of American literature at Stendhal University-Grenoble, France. He is the author of a book on Nelson Algren and has published articles on American literature in French, Serbian, Slovenian, Indian, and American scholarly publications. He has published "Trout Fishing and Woodworking: Digression in Percival Everett's *Erasure*" (in *Percival Everett: Transatlantic Readings*, edited by Claire Maniez and Anne-Laure Tissut).

SARAH MANTILLA GRIFFIN received her B.A. with honors from Stanford University in 2004 and her Ph.D. from the University of Pennsylvania in 2012. Her research and teaching interests include African American literature, literature and theory of the African diaspora, black feminist theory, sound theory, and world literature. Sarah's dissertation, entitled "'Hush Now Can You Hear It': Black Women's Sonic Literature," contributes to recent critical discourses of American modernism and sonic modernity through an exploration of the various sounds of black women's twentieth- and twenty-first-century writing.

KEITH B. MITCHELL is Associate Professor of English at the University of Massachusetts at Lowell. He is the coeditor of *After the Pain: Critical Essays on Gayl Jones* and coeditor of the *Xavier Review* special issue "Reading the Intersections of Sex and Spirit in the Creative Arts." Mitchell has published book chapters, articles, and reviews in *Obsidian III: Literature in the African Disapora*, *The Oxford Companion to African American Literature*, *Southern Writers: A New Biographical Dictionary*, *The Bryn Mawr Review of Comparative Literature*, *Oyster Boy Review*, and other publications. Forthcoming projects include a monograph on the fiction of Percival Everett and a book-length study of the intersections of the African American and the Jewish Diasporas in contemporary Anglophone and Francophone Caribbean literature.

RICHARD SCHUR is an Associate Professor of English and the director of the Law and Society Program at Drury University. He is the author of *Parodies of Ownership: Hip-Hop Aesthetics and Intellectual Property Law* and coeditor of *African American Culture and Legal Discourse*. His research focuses on African American culture, popular music, and law.

ANTHONY STEWART is a Professor in the English department at Dalhousie University. His main research interest is in twentieth- and twenty-first-century African American literature and culture, and he also teaches twentieth-century British literature. He is the author of *George Orwell,*

Doubleness, and the Value of Decency and *You Must Be a Basketball Player: Rethinking Integration in the University.* His current research includes editing a special collection of the *Canadian Review of American Studies* on the work of Percival Everett, a critical book on Percival Everett, tentatively titled *Approximate Gestures: The Infinity of Bothness in Percival Everett's Fiction,* and a book-length personal essay, tentatively titled *Confessions of a Middle-Class Black Man: How We Think About Privilege.*

SARAH WYMAN is an Assistant Professor at the State University of New York at New Paltz where her research examines poetics and the visual arts. She has published in *CLCWeb: Comparative Literature and Culture* and *Word & Image: A Journal of Verbal/Visual Enquiry.* Forthcoming articles on rhetorics of representation in U.S. literature are to be published in *The Comparatist, ANQ: A Quarterly Journal of Short Articles, Notes and Reviews* and *Amerikastudien/American Studies.* Her poem, "Message," will appear in *Mudfish.*

ROBIN G. VANDER is an Assistant Professor in the Department of English at Xavier University of Louisiana. Her research areas are performance studies, African Diaspora studies, and the poetics of anthropology including ethnography and narratives of social justice. With Keith B. Mitchell, she is the coeditor of the *Xavier Review* (2007) special issue exploring the intersections of spirituality and sensuality, and has served as guest editor for a special issue of *The Review of Black Political Economy* (2011) examining post-Katrina recovery in New Orleans. Her work has also been published in *The Oxford Companion to African American Literature, The Greenwood Encyclopedia of African American Literature,* and *Nature of a Sistah: Black Women's Lived Experiences in Contemporary Culture.*

Index

Page numbers in **bold** reference illustrations.

jazz, 102; African Americans and, 96–
97; improvisation in, 102–3. *See also*
Suder: jazz in; *Suder*: "Ornitholo-
gy" in
Johnson, Charles: *Dreamer*, 76; *The Ox-
herding Tale*, 76
Johnson, E. Patrick, 12
Johnson, James Weldon, "The White
Witch," 135
Jones, LeRoi, 95; *Blues People: Black Mu-
sic in White America*, 104

Kazin, Alfred, 68–69
Keb' Mo', "Dirty, Low Down and Bad,"
97–98
Kincaid, Jim, 131
King, Larry, 19
Komunyakaa, Yusef, "Anodyne,"
134–35
Kristeva, Julia, 29

Lacan, Jacques: forclusion, 20, 22,
33n5; Name-of-the-Father, 23; "The
Psychoses," 21–22, 33n1; relation to
one's own body and, 28–29; signification and, 22, 23, 27; soul murder
and, 30; theory of lack, 20
Larsen, Nella, *Quicksand*, 37
Lillies of the Field, 27

Madison, D. Soyini, 151n3
maenads, 41
Magritte, René, "Ceci n'est pas une
pipe," 6
Marshall, Paule, *Brown Girl, Brownstones*, 37
Marx, Groucho, 94
Marx, Leo, 70; *Machine in the Garden*,
62; *The Pilot and the Passenger*, 62

McKay, Claude, *Home to Harlem*, 37
mind-body split, 75. *See also* African
American literary tradition: mind-
body split and; *American Desert*:
mind-body split and; *Erasure*: mind-
body split in; Everett, Percival:
mind-body split and; *I Am Not Sidney Poitier*: mind-body split and
Mitchell, Keith, 17n1, 135
Morgan, J. P., 69
Moynihan, Daniel Patrick, *The Negro
Family: The Case for National Action*,
34n9
Muir, John, 71, 74n4
Murray, Albert, 97

nature writing, 61
New Black Aesthetic, 76
Nobus, Dany, 33n1
Nouryeh, Andrea J., "Soyinka's Eurip-
ides: Postcolonial Resistance or
Avant-Garde Adaptation," 44

Obama, Barack, 77
Okpewho, Isidore, "Soyinka, Euripides,
and the Anxiety of Empire," 40
Orwell, George, 113
Ouspensky, P. D., *The Fourth Way*, 58n5

Parker, Charlie "Bird," 101; "Ornitholo-
gy," 96, 101, 102, 119. *See also Suder*:
"Ornithology" in
Patterson, Orlando, 24
performance, 139–40, 144–45. *See also
For Her Dark Skin*: performance and
performative writing, 141–42, 147,
148–49
Petry, Anne, 94
Plato, "Allegory of the Cave," 5–7, 89

www.ingramcontent.com/pod-product-compliance
Lightning Source LLC
Chambersburg PA
CBHW020658030726
47498CB00002B/567